# Raising Sc
# Infancy to Adulthood:
## Preparing Our Children for College and Demolishing Prison Walls

Dr. James C. Brown
Dr. M. Jamal Colson
Dr. Lynn B. Elfe
Dr. Michelle Gantt

# Raising Scholars from Infancy to Adulthood:
## Preparing Our Children for College and Demolishing Prison Walls

# Table of Contents

# Chapter 1:
# Introduction

We are scholars. The four of us—Drs. Brown, Colson Elfe, and Gantt—have our own individual story of how we arrived here. There are some differences in our stories, but the similarities are many. When we asked ourselves if we were first-generation college graduates (neither parent having a bachelor's degree), three of us answered yes. When we asked if we had come from meager backgrounds, two of us answered yes and the other two explained that they were middle class. One of the scholars who mentioned being from a meager background stated "I didn't know we had a meager background until later in life. Our parents made the best of a little and still had their children excel academically." We believe you can do this too!

Another question we asked ourselves was whether we had access to mentors. All but one of us answered in the affirmative. One of the scholars explained, "I've had mentors and have identified traits and behaviors in family members that I admired." When we thought about parental support, we asked if our parents were supportive in our academic endeavors. Again we all answered in the affirmative. Another scholar responded saying, "There was never a doubt in my mind that I was going to college. My dad let me know early on that college was as basic as high school and both my parents did whatever they needed to help me make it happen." If you are not doing this for your children, you can start today.

There is an underlying theme about who we are. We are Black scholars who were supported through our education and accepted the challenges and adversity to reach our goals. We also care about parents trying to educate their children. We want readers to understand that no matter what your background is the level of education you completed, the income category you fall into, or the zip code you live in, you can still raise your children to become scholars.

We do not want you to think the process is always easy but we do want you to know that it is possible. When we asked ourselves why we wanted to write this book, one of the scholars explained, "I want the young men and women from underprivileged areas to know they can make it." Another scholar said, "I wanted to write this book to help parents raise scholars, because it's possible. I want to bridge the academic achievement gap. I want every parent . . . who wants more for their children to be able to give more to them . . . they [parents] can begin to understand that regardless of where they start they can finish with scholars."

Who are we as scholars? We are educators who met in our doctoral program. As we progressed through the program we realized that we believed in the same issues. Although our focus has been on the different grade levels of education, we knew we wanted the elimination of the achievement gap. We knew we wanted children to be able to move through grades having access to all education can offer, with an opportunity to explore a prosperous future completing college and to achieve beyond the degree.

Each of us had supportive people in our lives who had expectations for us that only education could fulfill. These people helped to create dreams for us. We completed the dream and we want many others to follow theirs.

As scholars, we have experiences we want to share. We have identified, researched, and undergone practices that we hope parents adopt, even though they may not think they have the ability, the means, the energy, the motivation, or the belief that they can help a child succeed academically. We want all parents to finally realize they can prepare their children to do well in education. We want to impart information to let them know they can create scholars and prevent their children from experiencing the prison system.

One of the scholars stated, "I want to share what I have learned in the last three and half-decades through experience research, and study. I want to provide information to parents who may not know what took me so long to learn on my own." We are scholars who want to make a difference. We have a dream for the future and in this vision our readers' children are the ones who will make the difference for a more educated country.

We want parents to confront the brutal facts of their

children's educational reality. We want to let the parents know they can be the positive impact on their children's future and that they can be the foundation to shorten that academic achievement gap and that they can aspire to produce scholars.

Yes, we the authors have more education than the average American. Yes, by the mere fact that the four of us have pursued and attained doctoral degrees means that we enjoy learning or understood that the degree would gain us access to further our careers. Each of us has realized the dream our parents had for us. We have more financial prosperity than our parents. We each own a house, a secure pension for retirement, and a set of skills and knowledge that we can market to produce our own income. Did this start with college graduation following high school? Yes it did; however, allow us to share more countrywide statistics.

Using the 2009 United States Census Bureau data, the average American without a high school diploma earns a little over $20,000 per year. This figure increases to a little over $30,000 per year for high school graduates. Americans who started college but did not finish earn a little more than $32,000 per year. Americans who earned a bachelor's degree earn a little more than $56,000 per year. As the level of education increases so does the average annual earnings.

Most people that we have talked to throughout our professional lives will freely admit they want their children to graduate from college because they understand the connection between average annual income and college graduation. What our scholarship has focused on is why certain groups of people who understand this connection still have difficulty graduating from college. If we look at completion rates of college by race and ethnicity, we see that 69% of Asian and Pacific Islander students that start college graduate with a bachelor's degree in six years; 62% of White students graduate with a bachelor's degree in six years; 50% of Hispanic students graduate with a bachelor's degree in six years while; 39% of Black or American Native graduate with a bachelor's degree in six years. Family wealth explains much of the difference between who starts college and who doesn't but wealth does not explain all of the difference. Black students coming from homes with the same family wealth as their White and Asian classmates are attaining college degrees at lower rates.

Tuition and fees for colleges and universities are often high and discourage many families from the pursuit of college graduation. Even attending the less expensive public universities do not remedy this academic achievement disparity as larger percentages of Black, Hispanic, or Native American students attend these institutions, but a smaller percentage persist until they receive their bachelor's degree when compared to their same race peers who attend more competitive and more expensive private universities and colleges.

Many Asian and Pacific Islander students have the same financial struggle as their Black, Hispanic, and Native American students face. There has been lots of research around the cultural differences that Asian students have regarding their relationships with their parents and teachers when compared to students from other races. These differences may explain the disparities in perceived work ethic, perceived effectiveness of parental supervision, and the perceived ability of students to form more effective relationships with teachers. There has been emerging research on the effect of American societies' stereotypes of Asian students and its relationship to higher expectations among teachers. These factors may contribute to the explanation for the success of many Asian Americans. The lessons that all people can learn from examining the academic and professional success of Asian Americans is that there is no substitute for high expectations and a commitment demonstrated by time and persistence. The expectations of Asian American parents are often concrete and measured by grades and transcripts. In these households, college graduation is not a pie-in-the-sky dream but a well-calculated plan that begins with the birth of their child.

Stereotypes about certain races and classes of people do affect expectations among educators in all levels. While we along with thousands of other educators from all types of races and class backgrounds work to eliminate this fact, parents have the ultimate responsibility and power to ensure that this does not negatively affect their children. Through daily communications, emotional support, teaching and mentoring children about the greatness of their heritage and struggle, as well as effective advocacy, parents can reduce the effects of stereotypes. Addressing the areas identified that are associated with race and class will allow their children to demonstrate their abilities and to achieve to the academic levels that guarantee a bachelor's degree.

The reality of the 21st-century global economy has made college graduation mandatory if first-generation college bound students want a life more prosperous than their parents. Typically it's not the children who have this forward thinking, it's their parents. The reason we are writing this book is to assist those parents who want a better life for their children.

We want to let parents know they cannot leave the education of their children up to schools. We want parents to know their capability. We want to let them know that they do have an impact on the educational possibilities of their children. The point we want to make to our readers is that no matter what the statistics may be today, they have the possibility of changing the numbers for tomorrow.

Anyone who is reading this book has the capability to make a difference in the educational lives of children. We want our readers to recognize that it takes time, attention, intention and love to create a scholar. Utilizing the information that is incorporated in this book will help all readers begin to see the scholar development process.

We want the readers to know that we have to make a change in order to boost test scores and create better educational foundations. Parents will need to change or enhance their educational expectations for their children. It is important for parents to understand their role as an educator in their children's life. This change can begin, one child at a time, one household at a time, one school district at a time. The point is that you can begin to make the change today.

Being first-generation college graduates, Doctors Brown Colson, Elfe, and Gantt experienced many of the same struggles and triumphs that you and your children may be experiencing together. Through our personal and professional experiences and our research findings we have found that high-achieving students and college graduates have parents that have concrete expectations for high achievement and college graduation. These parents match these expectations with a set of practices that develop their children into successful students. Knowing the difference between abstract and concrete expectations and doing these special parental practices, we are convinced that anyone can raise a scholar from infancy to adulthood.

If our children are to have meaningful participation in the 21st-century global economy, we are required to raise them as scholars. While having family wealth does help, there are many children who live in poverty that overcome that circumstance and experience both financial and personal prosperity. If you implement our research-based strategies within your family, you will improve your communication with your child, create a true commitment to setting goals, work smart and hard, as well as increase your child's academic and professional success.

While we hear many stories about people who lacked a college degree but still became personally and financially prosperous, what we often do not hear is how many of these people began with more family wealth and access to a network of vital information. If you can provide your child with these two resources, the practices that we are recommending may not be necessary. However, the vast majority of us do not start our adult lives with wealth and a network of people who can introduce our children to the right situations and the right people at the right time. A college degree, and a plan on how to leverage this piece of paper, is still the best strategy for the vast majority of Americans to improve their lives.

As you read this book, we want you to try our suggestions. *Raising Scholars from Infancy to Adulthood* is written for you to begin setting concrete expectations regardless of how old your child or children may be. There are too many children who are adversely affected by incarceration and so we have written a section for incarcerated parents. While in some communities single-parent households have become the norm our experiences reinforced with our research findings revealed that having two parents working together is far more effective than one. Parenting is not easy. Parenting is not a task on a "To Do" list to be completed as quickly as possible. Parenting is forming a lifelong relationship, sometimes with a person who doesn't want it but always needs it. It is our hope that when you read this book, we have increased your inspiration to dedicate more time and energy to raising your child to become a scholar. Additionally, incorporating the strategies and concepts presented will enhance your parental knowledge as well as your role as an educator in your child's life.

# Chapter 2:
# Pre-school Parenting Practices

# Dr. James C. Brown

The happiest moment of many people's lives is the first time they see and hold their baby son or daughter. Almost all parents fantasize about the aspirations and dreams this young life will lead. Amidst all the joy and happiness, parents of a newborn must begin a new chapter in their lives, a chapter that is dedicated to putting the children before their own needs and desires. The selflessness that is required in order to ensure that your child will achieve the dreams that he or she has for himself or herself and that you have for your child as his or her parent begins before the baby is born. Expectant mothers must take advantage of all the prenatal health opportunities they can afford. There are many prenatal health programs to ensure that your baby will be born healthy. Good nutrition and regular exercise and play will ensure that your child is ready to embark on a journey to becoming a scholar. While listing all of these programs is outside the scope of this book, the authors encourage all expectant mothers to engage in healthy behaviors and to take advantage of prenatal healthcare.

Fathers, extended family members, and friends of the expectant mother can also help in the creation of a scholar. Fetuses respond to love and language. Talking to the belly of the expectant mother is a healthy and effective pre-school practice of parents of future scholars. Language should not include just adult words but also include lyrical and poetic content, as well as baby talk.

Soon after the trip home and when family and friends leave parents are faced with their newfound job, raising this young prince or princess into a scholar. The effort that goes behind raising a baby is often viewed as the drudgery of changing diapers, sleepless nights, and guaranteeing that the basic requirements for human survival are met. While these tasks are of utmost importance, the job of preparing a newborn baby for school is often neglected. The most important job a human being can be employed in is being a parent. Not only is being a good parent an investment in your child's future but it is also an investment in yours.

In 2006, as high as 33% of mothers who have school-aged children contributed either time or money to their parents' or in-laws' households. This contribution increases as older parents begin their lives on fixed incomes. As people begin to live longer the percentage of what is known as the sandwich generation (adults who are financially supporting and caring for both their school aged children and their aging parents) will surely increase. It is well worth the investment of time to plan and participate in games with newborn babies that allow these infants to learn and explore the world around them. Children who receive hugs, praises, and coddling regularly from their parents begin to associate those good feelings with love and satisfaction. Parents to newborns must respond to the needs their children expressed vocally. This responsiveness will encourage infants to continue to utilize language to articulate their needs, a skill that ensures academic success in both secondary and post-secondary education.

Many people may feel having a child accompany you on errands such as going to the grocery store, picking up dry cleaning, or going to the bank is fraught with minor annoyances such as securing strollers and car seats, or dressing babies appropriately for the weather. These activities allow your child to learn about the world around them and will pay dividends later in school. Education, even as early as pre-kindergarten is built on a student's prior knowledge. As soon as a baby is born, prior knowledge is being constructed.

The first 2 years of human life marks the greatest growth that a human being will ever have. During this time, the child's first and most important teachers, his or her parents, teach vital language and social skills. Often times the achievement gap between students will find its roots in the activities and resulting skills that occurred in the child's first few years of life.

Clark (1983) found the differences between the pre-school parental practices of the successful and unsuccessful students were the teaching of social skills necessary for school success and the monitoring of television watching. Parents of unsuccessful and successful students read to their pre-school children. However, Hart and Risley (2003) conducted several at-home observations, and found that by the age of three, there could be a 30-million word difference in a child's vocabulary depending on the socioeconomic status (SES) of their parents. Even among children of parents who had the same income or same occupation, a gap would exist if the parents utilized the same or similar practices their parents used. The ratios between encouraging words to prevention words differ among parents:

- Parents who are professionals on average use 32 encouraging words compared to five prevention words
- Parents who are not professionals but work full time on average use 12 encouraging words compared to seven prevention words
- Parents who are receiving public assistance use five encouraging words compared to 11 prevention words.

Parents typically learn how to parent or not parent from their own parents. Among parents with the same occupation and annual income, but different vocabulary resources, the "word gap" may exist. The "word gap" reflects the difference in the number of different words used per hour, the average utterances per hour, and the recorded vocabulary size of children from different socio-economic backgrounds. The children's levels were highly correlated to their parents' level of educational attainment (Hart & Risley, 2003). Depending on the grandparents' educational attainment, middle-class children may enter school with differences in their vocabulary resources and their language and interaction styles (Phillips, Brooks-Gunn, Duncan, Klebanov & Crane, 1998).

High academic achievement begins with parents having expectations that their 3-year olds follow household routines. These expectations for pre-schoolers include children taking responsibility for cleaning their eating area, putting their jackets or coats away, and pouring their own water. Some thought has to go into arranging your household so that your 3- and 4-year-old can do these tasks independently. Having these expectations for your children prepares you for developing concrete expectations for high academic achievement. Supervising the activities demonstrates that these expectations are being met. It also prepares your child to anticipate your expectations and supervision of their activities. When children complete these tasks they should be showered with praise to positively reinforce their actions. It will take longer for your child to complete these tasks independently than it would if you help them or do it for him or her. You must resist the temptation to allow your busy schedule to interfere with the time required to supervise and ensure your 3- or 4-year-old child completes their assigned tasks.

Most public schools require students to master routines almost immediately. By establishing routines in your household for your pre-school children you are preparing them for success in public school. Because of the nature of public schools successful students will have to master going from one task to another. One of the challenges that you will face is resisting the temptation to complete tasks for your children, especially when they need to transition from play or leisure time to get ready to accompany you on trips outside of the house. It is important to take the time to teach your child how to make these transitions smoothly. Be patient, do not allow yourself to become frustrated and do not give in to your child by completing these tasks for him or her. Teaching children that you will not lower your expectation at this young age will pay dividends when you begin discussing grades and college admission.

Even if your child has no siblings, a priority of parents is to allow your child to learn the social skills that will be required as scholars. Part of the job as a parent is to introduce and nurture friendships with children of similar age, if not the same age, as your 3- or 4-year-old. Providing opportunities for play dates to occur both in and outside the household is one of your most important tasks. Skills such as teamwork and conflict resolution, which are all important school success skills that your child must master, are acquired during these play dates. At age three, children often know the difference between good and bad decisions. Parents must teach their children to self-regulate their behavior and must not hesitate to teach and discipline when children continue to do the wrong things.

Not only are you allowing your child to practice social skills and language, if play dates are done often enough, you should begin to build trust and confidence in the parenting skills of other parents. When you need to recharge your own battery through time away from your child, you will be able to because you have developed a friendship with other parents as a result of these play dates.

The achievement gap between Black and White children exists regardless of household income. This means that Black children in the most well-funded public schools in the most exclusive neighborhoods are still performing at lower levels than White students. Logically, one would conclude that pre-school practices contribute to this gap but the question remains which practices contribute the most? In a National Center for Education Statistics (O'Donnell, 2008) report on school readiness, parents reported reading, telling stories, and teaching the letters of the alphabet, basic sight words, the numbers 1–10, songs, and music to their pre-school children. Here are some surprising facts from the report:

- Sixty-seven percent of Asian and Black students are enrolled in day care, pre-school, pre-kindergarten, or Head Start while 62 % of White students are enrolled
- The percentage of Black parents who reported their child could recognize all letters and read written words was higher than White parents
- A higher percentage of Black parents engage in reading comprehension activities with their pre-school children compared to parents of other sub-groups.

The NCES study also measured the beliefs of parents about children's pre-school academic abilities. Here are some of those beliefs:

- White parents believed their pre-school children could write their first name, count to 20 or higher, and their children's speech could be heard and understood by others at slightly higher percentages than Black parents

- Asian parents report the highest percentage of school readiness skills among all races except holding a pencil with fingers where their reported percentage is slightly lower than White parents
- The percentage of Hispanic parents that reported their child's readiness for school was lowest among all sub-groups
- A smaller percentage of Asian, Black, and Hispanic parents believed it was essential for their children to know these school readiness skills when compared to White parents.

With these statistics, it would seem that Asian, Black and White children are engaged in very similar pre-school practices but here are the two most interesting statistics of the report:

- The percentage of Asian and White parents who read to their children daily is about double the percentage of Black and Hispanic parents
- Black parents of preschoolers allowed 3.1 hours of television watching on weekdays and 3.3 hours on weekend days compared to Asian and White parents who allowed 2.2 and 2.4 hours during the week respectively and 2.6 hours during weekends. Hispanic parents allowed 2.7 hours during the week and 2.6 hours during the weekend.

The NCES report indicated that Black parents were reporting implementation of higher rates of particular pre-school practices each time they read or spent structured time with their children when compared to the number of times other parents read to their children or spent structured time with their children. Black parents reported reading less frequently with their pre-school children when compared to the number of times Asian and White parents read to their children or the number of hours they spent with their children in less structured time.

During the time this data was collected and still true during when the authors wrote this book, Black and Hispanic families have less wealth than White families. Families with less wealth but similar annual income usually required more hours of work outside the household from both parents. Black and Hispanic families must figure out how to spend more time reading to their pre-school children and allow these same children to spend less time watching television. This time must come from somewhere. Since Blacks and Hispanics need to work more hours outside the household to maintain the same income as Whites, decisions need to be made in terms of having less annual income or having less leisure time.

When compared to the percentage of White parents who believe that school staff should teach their children the alphabet sharing, reading, the recognition and recitation of the first ten numerals, and holding a pencil properly, the percentage of Asian Black and Hispanic parents believed that school staff should teach these school-readiness skills was higher (O'Donnell, 2008). These differences reflect a dissimilar belief about the role of school among different groups of parents; however, these beliefs translated into pre-school practices that also precipitate the achievement gap between Black and White students (Clark 1983; Phillips et al., 1998; Hart & Risley, 2003).

"Fifteen-year-old students whose parents often read books with them during their first year of primary school show markedly higher scores" is a statement in a 2009 report on the Program for International Student Assessments (PISA) sponsored by the Organisation for Economic Co-Operation and Development (2010). PISA is a set of examinations that students of the same age take in different countries. These examinations allow American students to be compared to Japanese, Swedish, Singaporean, and many other countries' students. When compared to students whose parents read with them infrequently or not at all, the performance advantage among students whose parents read to them in their early school years is evident regardless of the family's socioeconomic background. For instance, the PISA (Organisation for Economic Co-Operation and Development, 2010) study revealed that "students whose parents reported that they had read a book with their child 'every day or almost every day' or 'once or twice a week' during the first year of primary school" have markedly higher scores in PISA 2009 program than students whose parents reported that they had read a book with their child "never or almost never" or only "once or twice a month." On average, the score difference on the PISA is 25 points. The PISA study noted, "on average, the score point difference in reading that is associated with parental involvement is largest when parents read a book with their child when they talk about things they have done during the day, and when they tell stories to their children." The score point difference is smallest when parental involvement takes the form of simply playing with their children.

The importance of parents teaching their children academic and social skills as well as responsibility and work ethic prior to the first days of school makes a large difference in the development of scholars. When you find out that you are having a baby, you fantasize about what that child will become. That fantasy must include raising a scholar and it begins with you becoming a dedicated and skilled teacher. You cannot expect someone else to do this work for you. It is solely your responsibility to prepare your child to get the most out of school.

# Chapter 3:
## Elementary School Practices

## Dr. M. Jamal Colson

Although most professionals in the field of education are in agreement that parent involvement is valuable, educators have not figured out the best ways to optimize this resource. Chavkin and Williams (1993) looked at parent involvement as an integral part of school reform. They saw parents and educators as having equally important demanding but different roles in children's education. In order to succeed in both their roles they needed to keep the necessary close communication.

The fact that you are reading this book is encouraging for two reasons. First, you care about your children. Second, you want to improve your parental practices. In order to raise a scholar, parents need to actively engage in the practices of instruction, modeling, reinforcement, and encouragement. This chapter will focus on these four pivotal practices of researched parental involvement practices that have been successful.

This chapter will seek to help you answer these essential questions:

- How well do you know your children?
- What kind of parental practices you should be engaged in at home?
- How are you assisting your children's education in school?
- What kind of guidance are you providing in their lives?

The research of these parental practices was developed from the theories and research of Hoover-Dempsey & Sandler (2005) and Colson (2010). These dimensions support children in the educational process.

## How Well Do You Know Your Children?

My research has led my interest to helping parents raise scholars. A significant question within that task is asking parents how well they know their children. Also pertinent to that inquiry is helping parents to understand how necessary it is for them to spend time with their children. Obviously, we live in a very fast-paced society in which we have access to multiple modes of information (cell phones, texting, email, Internet etc.). We are open and available to the world in ways we've never been before; however, we are also distracted. A sick day, a day off or vacation, even an ordinary evening at home is not the same as it was years ago. By staying constantly connected to all that is accessible, it is easy to unintentionally neglect the immediate needs our children may have. It's important that parents use those skills that are necessary for them to be successful in their jobs and careers. However, that same deliberation applies with raising a scholar. Parents would do well to commence and maintain conversations, interactions and purposeful connections with their children. This is so vital and important because parents will begin to understand how their children see and process the world. Children want to share during the elementary years. This is how they begin to process their environment. If we're not spending time with them we could be missing crucial opportunities, and more importantly missing the opportunity of learning how we can best support their curiosity.

As a parent, teacher, and administrator, I work with students and parents daily from sunrise to sunset. I am privy to the cares and concerns of my students. When was the last time your children shared a dream with you? Have you inquired lately? When was the last time your children shared an aspiration? How did you respond? I remember asking my 4-year-old and youngest child what she wanted to become when she got older and she replied "a teenager." I was hoping to hear that she aspired to become a doctor, lawyer, judge, or accountant instead. It's important to understand your children's developmental stage. Most children at the age of four are not thinking about adulthood. Parents are wise to remember that children crawl before they walk.

One of the reasons I mention dreams is because this becomes an opportunity for elementary-age children to use their imaginations with respect to the future. As I discuss "dreams" it is in the context of goals and visions. As I work with young students, I find that many do not have their futures in mind. Some have very limited goals, visions, and aspirations. I am not implying that children need to walk around with their resume in one hand and a business plan in the other. Children benefit tremendously from exploring their creativity.

As a parent you might find it helpful to explore Howard Gardner's multiple intelligence theory. Howard Gardner (1985) claims that all human beings have multiple intelligences. These intelligences can be nurtured and strengthened, or ignored and weakened. He believes each individual has nine intelligences I listed eight:

- **Verbal-Linguistic Intelligence**
Example: well-developed verbal skills and sensitivity to the sounds, meanings, and rhythms of words
- **Mathematical-Logical Intelligence**
Example: ability to think conceptually and abstractly, and the capacity to discern logical or numerical patterns
- **Musical Intelligence**
Example: ability to produce and appreciate rhythm, pitch, and timber
- **Visual-Spatial Intelligence**
Example: capacity to think in images and pictures, to visualize accurately and abstractly
- **Bodily-Kinesthetic Intelligence**
Example: ability to control one's body movements and to handle objects skillfully
- **Interpersonal Intelligence**
Example: capacity to detect and respond appropriately to the moods, motivations, and desires of others
- **Intrapersonal Intelligence**
Example: capacity to be self-aware and in tune with inner feelings, values, beliefs, and thinking processes

- **Naturalist Intelligence**
Example: ability to recognize and categorize plants animals, and other objects in nature.

Research suggests that most jobs that current elementary age children will have as adults have not been created yet. For instance, during the early years 2000's colleges were not preparing students for the type of security that is now needed since 9/11. This single event has changed daily life as we know it; hence the creation of an extension to the executive branch of the American government entitled: Homeland Security. The take home point here is that as the world evolves, its evolution becomes more apparent. Raising a scholar will lead your child through the evolutionary changes within employment. As parents we need to know our children and help them reach their dreams, goals, and aspirations. In this way we will be able to assist our scholars in identifying the global changes, which lead them to a desired end.

Taking responsibility of our children is vital. We cannot merely rely upon the school systems or influential people to educate our children. To lead as role models, we parents need to begin with ourselves. Parents need to walk the walk as we talk the talk of academic success. If you did not reach a certain desired level of academic success, we are writing to encourage you so that your children can and may do so through these researched based practices. Continue to read and discover how you can accomplish great things for yourself and your children. Parental involvement through modeling leads to instruction, which fosters encouragement, which promotes reinforcement:

Modeling + Instruction + Encouragement + Reinforcement = Scholar   (M + I + E + R = Scholar)

In my experience as an elementary school assistant principal, I would often converse with teachers who claim that they would not be able to contact parents; especially those of children who were really in need of support and guidance in academic language. Many teachers would report that since the child came to school without their homework completed, they assumed that the parent was not involved. I discovered the opposite. In addition to my personal experience, and while in pursuit of research on how to raise a scholar, my findings were that parents of less proficient students spend more time talking about television shows and events of their day while the parents of high-achieving children tend to talk about future events and college. Parents of high-achieving students spend less time talking about homework partially because these students can complete the homework without supervision. Parents whose children are less proficient report that they do not understand the homework so they send the child to school to learn, as opposed to sending them to school to have the teacher penalize the child for not understanding the material.

Parents in low-income communities vary considerably in their beliefs about supporting their child's education. Some low-income parents do not see their role as active school involvement and believe schooling is best left up to teachers (Lareau, 1989). While other parents take a far more active role in the schooling process.

It is important to find out the type of learners your children are. Some examples of the types of learning styles are auditory, a preference of learning by hearing; visual, a preference for what they can see; and tactile learning, the preference for what they can feel. There are various strategies associated with each of these learning styles:

The Auditory Learner

Some strategies that help support this learning style are the use of CDs, listening to audio books, and listening to classroom instruction after class is over. These tactics will help your child fill in the gaps in addition to studying their written notes. After your children have read something, summarize it and recite it aloud together.

Visual Learner

Parents should make sure their children read over all study materials. Additionally, they should access charts, maps notes, and visual aids such as PowerPoint slides. They should practice visualizing or picturing words and concepts in their minds. They should write notes for frequent and quick visual review.

Tactile Learner

The parents of younger children in this group should make sure they trace words after they are written. Facts that must be learned should be written several times. Keep a supply of paper for this purpose. Using word applications on the computer is extremely helpful for this type learner. Taking and keeping lecture notes will be a very important step as well as making study sheets.

To raise a scholar is like planting a vineyard, the more knowledgeable you are of soil, seasons, weather, environment and especially grapes, the greater the opportunity for a fine wine. In raising a scholar it's important to keep this concept in mind as you plan toward your child's future. All the information in this book should be completed with purpose, just as a wine grower arranges the vineyard based upon the right conditions for a particular grape, seeking to produce the best crop. Parents, you are making one of the greatest investments by choosing to raise children with a purpose and then choosing to intentionally raise a scholar. Parents' ability to understand their children's intelligence and learning style facilitates the educational process that leads to scholars.

## What Kind of Parental Practices Should You Engage in at Home?

Parental practices bring to mind my past coaching experiences. Coaching boys' and girls' basketball practices were challenging. As a coach I planned and prepared for each practice and game. I continually reminded myself that the game was reserved for the players because I would often find myself asking what happened to the team. They would practice at times like they had never been coached: no hustle, no aggressive defense. I would reinforce effort and attitude. Again, to be on my team they needed to cultivate consistent effort and a positive attitude. I didn't mind mistakes. What I did mind was lack of effort and a discouraging attitude. You could never predict how a practice session would end. Sometimes the session would start well and end on a bad note. Other times they would start out rough and end on an encouraging note. Parenting is similar to this coaching scenario. Some parental practices that you apply will find to be successful immediately. Other practices are going to ask more from you, wherein you may not be as successful so quickly. We encourage you to stay the course.

Your children are the players in the game of education. It's your responsibility to equip yourself with these effective strategies. The goal is to gain understanding that just as parents are consistent; the child will tend to be as well. As previously stated, parental involvement and positive modeling leads to instruction leading to encouragement, then reinforcement.

Parental practice of instruction refers to direct instruction. Direct instruction has to do with helping your children learn facts in a straightforward process. The practice of direct instruction is critical when choosing to raise a scholar. The ability to provide direct instruction for your children is an important parental choice.

To raise a scholar you need to offer an array of direct instruction for your children. Some examples of how parents can provide direct instruction are:

- Teaching children the importance of completing homework each night
- Insisting that children complete all of the work correctly and check over all assignments
- Teaching children daily on how important an education is to their future
- Teaching children on how important it is to have a positive attitude toward their education
- Teaching children on how important it is to strive for success in the things they attempt in their lives.

After reading these examples, you may be unsure on how much direct instruction to provide your elementary-aged child.

Parents should be teaching independence so this decision is tricky.

## Parental Involvement Practice of Reinforcement

Parental reinforcement is another practice that will lead to raising scholars. Reinforcement refers to those external "rewards" or behavioral contingencies that parents enact with the general intention of shaping the children's behavior to meet desired goals (Hoover-Dempsey & Sandler, 2005). Parents who are seeking to raise scholars need to reinforce the importance of academic and learning success. The key to reinforcement is figuring out what is important to your child. If you have more than one child, realize each child is different and will require different reinforcements. The one-size-fits-all approach does not apply in raising a scholar. What works for one child may not apply for all. Here are examples of reinforcement practices:

- I reinforce to my child that education is very important
- I reinforce to my child that homework is important by signing their agenda book every night from kindergarten throughout elementary school
- I reinforce to my child that it is essential to do a review of school work over a weekend
- I reinforce to our child that they are rewarded for doing well.

Here are possible rewards that parents can use to reinforce behaviors they expect from their children:

- Educational trips to library and museums
- Computer/video game time
- Board games played together as a family
- Dining out or preparing a meal together.

## Parental Involvement Practice of Modeling

The parental involvement practice of "modeling" was developed out of the modeling theory of Bandura (1994) that suggests that students learn in part by observing models. Modeling is especially effective when undertaken by adults particularly parents whose children are perceived to be responsive, competent, powerful, and accessible (Bandura, 1994). Hoover-Dempsey & Sandler (2005) found that parents' values toward education relate to their children's educational attainment, persistence, and performance. Parental involvement practice of modeling can also take the form of expectations for educational achievement. Students' perceptions of parental expectations have important effects on educational outcomes (Muller & Kerbow, 1993). Parents should ask themselves two basic questions: Am I modeling behavior that simply sets a good example, or, am I setting an example that will lead my child to be a scholar?

When it comes to the practice of modeling, parents can utilize the following examples:

- Taking the time and effort to teach my child to work independently, believing that has made my child more focused and organized with his/her school work
- Showing my child that school is top priority and extracurricular activities always come second
- Showing my child that if you do not strive for success in school you will most likely not strive for it later in life.

## Parental Involvement Practice of Encouragement

It is vital that parents take responsibility for their children. Parents cannot solely rely on the school systems or influential people to educate their children. Parental encouragement identifies that parents engage in activities with their children while encouraging the child's belief that his or her parents' behaviors, interests, and beliefs are conducive to academic achievement. This happens during a parental involvement activity, such as monitoring or helping the student with homework.

The theme of encouragement can be expressed in several ways if a parent wants to create a scholar. For example expanding knowledge, confidence, and taking responsibility are practices of encouragement. One parent expressed the theme as "I encourage confidence, and a 'don't give up' attitude." Another parent expressed encouragement as, "I will encourage him/her to be the best they can be." To raise a scholar parents need to provide an explicitly positive attitude toward educational goals. There are many things that parents may not be able to control. However, when it comes to encouragement, parents, you can provide it! Encouragement is an unlimited natural resource supplied to every parent with or without a college degree. Parents of high-achieving students from my research shared how they encouraged their child in school:

*I also encourage them to do their best and to push themselves to do their best. I am always available to their teachers, coaches, and others to discuss my child's progress. I also show by my example of achieving that they can do what they set their minds to do.*

*I encourage reading.*

*My child has a learning disability. She struggles with schoolwork so patience and time are what is important for me to give so she isn't overwhelmed.*

*I try to have him work in a quiet, well-lit and undisturbed location.*

*We do homework together as soon as they come home.*

*I check their homework with them to make sure everything is correct. In the mornings there is no television, or video games, or playing until the children are completely ready for school with their backpacks by the door.*

*On school nights the children read to us before they go to bed.*

*School and schoolwork take the highest priority over any other activities.*

*She is rewarded for doing well. Homework is done first then extracurricular activities are encouraged.*

*I encourage him to always do his best. College is always spoken about, we constantly speak about different career choices.*

*I am extremely involved in all my son's school and extracurricular activities. I feel that if he sees his parents showing support and enthusiasm it will encourage him to do the best he can. I also feel that it is extremely important for my child to know that I care about the things he cares about.*

*I encourage our child to learn all that they can.*

*I try to encourage my children to do their best and try their hardest.*

*I encourage studying hard, and encourage participation in class.*

## What Kind of Guidance Are You Providing in Their Lives?

According to Henderson and Mapp (2002), students with involved parents, regardless of their family's annual income or background were more likely to:

- Earn higher grades and test scores, and enroll in higher-level programs
- Be promoted, pass their classes, and earn credits
- Attend school regularly
- Have better social skills, show improved behavior and adapt well to school
- Graduate and go on to post-secondary education.

Henderson and Mapp also found that parents of all incomes education levels, ethnic, and cultural groups, are engaged in supporting their children's learning at home.

## Conclusion

This chapter has now begun to help you answer the essential questions concerning raising a scholar:

- How well do you know your children?
- What kind of parental practices you should be engaged in at home?
- How are you assisting your children's education in school?
- What kind of guidance are you providing in their lives?

Our aim in Raising Scholars from Infancy to Adulthood is to assist parents in raising a scholar. To do this we feel we must address the changes in the expectations that your child will be required to meet. New York State has joined 45 other states and adopted the Common Core State Standards initiative on July 19 2010. The State Education Department (SED) plans for full implementation during the 2013–2014 school years. Since the adoption, the SED has implemented 12 major "shifts" for classroom instruction, six shifts in English language arts and six shifts in mathematics (EngageNY, 2013). These changes in education are challenging not only for teachers and students but also for parents as well. The following bullets summarize the shifts in English language arts/Literacy and mathematics.

## English Language Arts/Literacy
- Read as much non-fiction as fiction
- Learn about the world by reading
- Read more challenging material
- Talk about reading using "evidence"
- Write about text using "evidence"
- Know more vocabulary

## Mathematics
- Build skills across grade levels
- Learn more about less
- Use math facts easily
- Think fast and solve problems
- Really know it, really do it
- Use math in the real world

I would like to bring you back to the beginning of the chapter where I stated "First, you care about your children and second you want to improve your parental practices." In order to raise a scholar, parents need to actively engage in the practices of instruction, modeling, reinforcement, and encouragement. In light of the instructional shifts resulting from the adoption of the Common Core State Standards, you can utilize these researched-based parental practices to assist your child in meeting these new expectations. The following are examples of activities parents can use to address the instructional shifts their children are experiencing.

| | Parental Involvement Practice | How Parents Can Assist Their Children |
|---|---|---|
| **ELA Shift** | | |
| Read more challenging materials | *Modeling* | Show that challenging books are worth reading |
| Write about text using "evidence" | *Encouragement* | Encourage writing at home |
| **Mathematics Shift** | | |
| Think fast and solve problems | *Instruction* | Instruct children to know, understand, and memorize basic math facts |
| Build skills across grade levels | *Reinforcement* | Reinforce the priority work at their grade level |

Of the four parental involvement practices (research-based practices) encouragement represents the strongest relationship between achievement and parental involvement practices. In the current education climate, many parents and teachers find themselves in separate worlds, often with parents maintaining a distinct "outsider" status. Given the factors that limit parent-teacher collaboration, it can seem that forging relationships with parents is too difficult to do. Yet teachers cannot fully achieve their professional goals without such help thus further reiterating the necessity of positive parent involvement practices.

# Chapter 4:
# Teenage Scholars

# Dr. James C. Brown

Raising children to be scholars is a time consuming task that requires just as much energy and intelligence as your company or job requires. Students just don't become scholars because you want them to; they become scholars because you raise them to be scholars. As parents, you must put in the time and energy that's required to support your children's academic achievement. This effort is only measured in success and takes the form of high-achievement supporting parental practices. The difference between a parent creating a scholar rather than an inmate has little to do with the statement "I care about my child's education." It has more to do with the effective practices behind that statement.

Teenagers can make your life miserable. You worked so hard taking care of them when they could not do anything for themselves. You became their personal chauffeurs when they needed transportation to all of the activities they participated in. You became their best friends when they had a rough day at school. You were their first teacher when you read their favorite story. Now, they are more interested in an ATM machine from the bank of parenthood that dispenses without any accountability. While this may seem unfair to you, it is the normal development of most of our teenagers.

Early teenage years mark the second most dramatic growth period in a human being's life. Dwarfed only by the rapid human development during the first 2 years of life, the early teenage years is a period where some boys want nothing to do with girls while others cannot keep their hands to themselves. This roller coaster ride for you marks the end of your reign of control. Ideas and feelings that may not agree with yours will emerge. There is a theory that uses an analogy to state that parents can stunt this growth making their children into lifetime consumers and employees or stimulate it, making them into owners, leaders, and employers.

Members of the 21st-century global society do not want a weak-minded individual telling them where to go or what to do in a crisis. In over 20 years of working with teenagers in schools I have seen the most rebellious and articulate individuals emerge as the leaders. At a time when children are beginning to determine who they will be as a man or woman, you must be careful not to squash this growth in attempt to remain in control. Now, I am not saying to allow your child to run "buck wild" but debate a little, give in sometimes, and enjoy the new adult friendship that will begin to emerge.


## Concrete Expectations

Knowing when you are being too hard or too easy is the artistic side of parenting. It starts with expectations. Too many low- and working-class parents of all races and first-generation college educated Black and Hispanic parents, expect their children's teachers to have expectations for college admission for their students; however, these parents do not meet the teachers' expectations for parents of college-bound students. Dr. Mickelson (1990) has a concept called "abstract and concrete attitudes." Abstract attitudes are nothing more than hope-on-a-stick. When I was a middle or high school principal, I usually asked a group of students, who were sent to me because they were misbehaving, if they wanted to go to college. They always said "yes"; but when we continued our discussion and we started looking at their last report card or their transcript we found neither earned credits nor final course grades that were higher than Cs. The declaration that these students made that they planned to attend college was an example of an abstract expectation. There was no plan, no research, and no knowledge of what it takes to go to college. This attitude was just a bunch of words that have no meaning because there was no effective parental supervision, parental follow up, or collaboratively planned action plan. There was not really a true belief about going to college in the future, just a hope, like our belief in wining the jackpot when playing the lottery. Too many of our children have abstract expectations. Only concrete expectations will allow our children to reach their goals.

So what are concrete expectations? They do start with the abstract expectation that your child must say "I want to go to college!" In a study by Downey, Ainsworth, and Qian (2009) they found these abstract attitudes did in fact predict high or low levels of academic achievement depending on what the student said he or she believed about education and its value for economic mobility. It's been my experience that most students understand that going to college will lead to a better life. When I speak to a group of Black males for the first time I always ask the question "How many of you are going to college?" It does not matter what grade level I'm talking to, 99% of the students answer in the affirmative "Yes, I am going to college." This response has its roots in both the societal and family influence. It is no doubt that the United States has done a great job of indoctrinating our children and parents to believe that college graduation will lead to economic mobility. The data is very clear on this. Those who attain higher degrees will earn higher incomes; however, the affirmation cannot stop here. The realm of concrete expectations takes this further and in my opinion is the difference between students attending colleges and universities and graduating from them.

Concrete expectations demonstrate a belief in the value of high academic achievement. A concrete expectation that a student will graduate from college is demonstrated by a work ethic to achieve specific grades. The higher the grades achieved the greater the value of the education in terms of earnings realized in the future of a child. How does this work? Higher grades and the ability to demonstrate mastery-level literacy and mathematics skills on standardized examinations allow students to gain admission in the more selective pre-secondary or secondary school, especially in large urban areas where specialized gifted and talented schools exist. Higher grades and the ability to demonstrate mastery-level literacy and mathematics skills on standardized examinations allow secondary students to gain admission in the more selective colleges and universities and to earn more scholarship money. Higher grades and the ability to demonstrate mastery-level literacy and mathematics skills on standardized examinations allow college and university graduates admission into the more selective medical, business, or law schools. These grades also improve young adult's chances of earning interviews and access to social networks that lead to more lucrative entrepreneurial opportunities, when most applicants have little or no work experience. The highly desired social network opportunities come from the possession of wealth or from high academic achievement. While too many lower achieving students and their parents do not know the relationship between future earnings and achievement levels, high-achieving students and their parents understand that high grades matter.

Most students do not perform poorly in school because they do not care about their academics; however, under-achieving students categorized their performance as being good without the influence of standardized test scores and teacher feedback at a greater frequency when compared to higher-achieving students. In other words, under-achieving students perceive themselves doing good work when their test results and teachers are saying something else. Too often, due to the past experiences of the Black students, their parents, and/or grandparents, valuable feedback from teachers is discounted. While it is important to protect Black children from the evils of racism and prejudice, Black parents must not forget to confront our children with the brutal facts of their current realities (Glasser, 1965). What I mean by that is simply not allowing your child to believe that the performance is good when it clearly is not. It is vital to explain to children that 75s and Cs or even 85s and Bs is just not good enough to meet their ultimate goals of becoming doctors, architects, lawyers, or engineers. What I see lacking through my conversations with lower achieving students and their parents is information on how higher levels of academic achievement can be leveraged into better financial outcomes.

When a sixth grader states, "I want to go to college," as a parent, the response needs to be "Wonderful, but what college do you want to go to?" Countless studies demonstrate Black students have high levels of self-esteem. Black parents have done a great job of ensuring that their children's self-worth is not connected to a society whose media depicts them as worthless and unfortunately dangerous. Black parents cannot be afraid to challenge their children because they think it's going to discourage or hurt his or her self-esteem. Pushing children of any race, when accompanied with strategic plans that have concrete objectives and the necessary information that makes this plan realistic and actionable, demonstrates to the child that having a plan and not settling and working just a little bit harder is a key to success in life. Once the plan is explained to children, the discussion on specific grades just becomes one part of this strategy. Conversations about children's academic performance will become more meaningful.

Teachers award grades to reflect the effort and achievement in their classrooms. Educators make all types of instructional decisions that affect your child using these grades. Grades also serve as a way to reward or punish students. Too many educators believe this is an effective motivation for students. Despite decades of failing grades with no real academic improvement for too many students, school systems continue to use grades for this purpose. I have personally seen teachers who were afraid of students feel a certain satisfaction giving failing grades. Instead, these same teachers need to feel that they have failed the student and his/her family each time they assign a failing grade. They need to adopt a professional responsibility for their students' achievement. In the current climate, teachers are under increasing pressure to align their grades to standardized tests. The days of teachers awarding a "nice" student (who does not misbehave, says "good morning" each day, and attempts to do their work), with an A, are dwindling. When this "nice" student receives an A but cannot achieve the highest levels on standardized tests or produce papers or projects that represent the Common Core Learning Standards for his/her grade, there will be problems for the teacher and the school.

Noted educator Robert Marzano (2000) found that the least important purpose for grades was communicating feedback about student achievement. This should be the most important purpose. There's a term known as "data-driven" or data-informed instruction. According to EngageNY (2013), this term is defined as a "precise and systematic approach to improving student learning throughout the year. The inquiry cycle of data-driven instruction includes assessment, analysis, and action." This practice of data-driven or data-informed instruction is recognized as a common best practice in the United States' most high-performing schools. Educators who use their students' standardized test scores, and their own analysis of classroom tests and assignments, as well as their observations to decide what to teach, how to teach it, and how much time students need to learn it are the ones who produce the highest level of achievement among their students. If these excellent schools and educators regularly practice using data to inform their instructional decisions, why shouldn't parents use their children's performance data to inform their parenting decisions?

## School Performance Discussions

To utilize discussions about a child's data to drive the decisions both you and your child will make, parents must understand the data that they can receive from schools. Most schools publish a calendar for the school year that details when you will receive report cards and progress reports. You must know these dates. You can post the dates on a refrigerator or some place else where you can be reminded when these reports will arrive.

In order for teachers to decide on the appropriate grades to give your child and later publish in the form of report cards or progress reports with comments, they must assess him or her frequently. At least once per week, you should ask your child for the results of an examination in each content area. Your daily conversations with your child should include:

- The learning that took place in school
- The homework that he or she has either completed or needs to complete
- The progress on any projects or papers that require sustained effort to finish.

These conversations should also include questions about the social interactions your child has engaged in during the course of the day. Andreas Schleicher, the deputy director of Education and Skills for the Organisation for Economic Co-operation and Development (the conductors of the Program of International Student Assessment, a series of examinations that compares students of the same ages attending schools in different countries) explained to Thomas Freidman (2011), the author of the best-selling book, *The World is Flat 3.0*, that "just asking your child how was their school day and showing genuine interest in the learning that they are doing can have the same impact as hours of private tutoring. It is something every parent can do, no matter what their education level or social background." Regardless of your educational level or social background, all parents can begin to joyfully engage in their child's learning process.

If you are reading this book, attending our presentations for the first time, or if you have not tried to engage your teenage child in these discussions about academic achievement performance before, you may only receive the NFO response. The NFO stands for "Nothing, Fine, or Okay." This response is unacceptable, as it does not provide you with the data that you need to inform you or your child's next decision. You need to find out the actual grades on tests, quizzes, term papers, or homework and projects returned. You need to find out if your child is not receiving homework or if they are not doing the homework. You need to find out how your child is doing on standardized examinations and if they need additional support so that they can improve their performance.

Your daily conversations about academic performance must result in actions, or these talks just end up being a bunch of words. Providing your children with praise and rewards when they meet the academic achievement goals has shown to be an effective parenting practice that results in high academic achievement.

**Inspect What You Expect**

Thomson, Hanson, and McLanahan (1994) studied parenting practices and achievement of students from ages 5 to 19. These authors defined parental control as the summary of the following:

- Amount of time children spent alone at home
- When that time alone occurred
- Television restrictions
- Rules about notifying parents of their child's whereabouts when that child was away from home.

Thomson, Hanson, and McLanahan defined family activities such as meals together, leisure time away from home, playing together, private conversations, help with homework, and participation in organized youth activities. The authors defined positive responses to children's behavior, such as praise and hugging, as parental practices that were found to support high academic achievement. Daily and weekly conversations must include discussions about parental control, family activities, and include positive responses.

Even when parents are engaging in effective parent control, participating in family activities, and positively responding to children's good decisions and successful academic and extracurricular endeavors, students will not be high achievers if they do not work hard or make sacrifices in their leisure time. Chores are excellent opportunities to measure children's willingness to make sacrifices and to work hard. The assignment of chores has been a social debate among social science researchers looking for answers on why certain kids achieve and others do not. Desimone (1999) found that the assignment of chores was not an effective practice that related to student achievement; while Mandura, Varner, Greene, and Richman (2009) found that it was. In my own study, the high-achieving Black males were assigned chores to complete.

In the book, *Top of the Class: How Asian Parents Raise*

*High Achievers—and How You Can Too*, Abboud and Kim (2006) shared their experiences with classmates and friends who had too many household responsibilities, particularly the raising of siblings, to dedicate enough time to become scholars. The authors of this book are advocating for the raising of scholars. They strongly believe parents' number one responsibility is to ensure that their children have the adequate resources to become high academic achievers. The most precious resource is time. All children need to have is adequate time to pursue high levels of academic achievement. As stated earlier, a parental activity known as control requires parents to monitor leisure time activities. The assignment of chores is just one way to ensure that students do not have too much leisure time. Children are taught a sense of responsibility when they are assigned tasks and are required to complete them.

Chores teach your children how to work hard and most do not require a great deal of difficult thinking. It is easy for you to judge your children's work ethic through chores. Dishes that are washed that still have dried food on them, beds that are made with clothes underneath the sheets, and rooms that are said to be clean without the removal of dust, dirt, and grime are examples of D's and F's for these tasks, and a demonstration of an inferior work ethic. The same shoddy dish-washer or room-cleaner is probably the child who believes two hours of daydreaming with notebooks and textbooks open is studying.

When class work becomes more difficult, particularly in the rigorous courses that scholars are required to enroll in, it is more difficult to judge your children's work ethic. It is unfair to state that your child is not working hard by examining their report cards or test grades when you know they have a strong work ethic demonstrated by the quality of their completed chores. When your children are assigned chores and complete them to your satisfaction then it is easier to rule out work ethic as the cause of low academic achievement. While the assignment of chores must not end with you doing the task for your child all the time, there should be an increase in study, practice, or sleep time if there is proper negotiation.

Once you are sure that your child knows how to work

hard, negotiating your completion of your child's chores becomes easier. This is about learning to trust your child and yourself as a parent. There will be times when your children need to ask you to complete an odd job for them and sometimes you must eventually agree to the request. Your child must be taught to negotiate. The discussion of chores is a great opportunity to teach this skill. Negotiation is a social skill that will serve your child well as they continue their lives outside the classroom. An immediate return on allowing your child to negotiate the chores is the mastery of the art of collaborating with teachers and other authority figures. High-achieving students know how to communicate with their teachers and are able to confer for additional time for assignments and additional support. Despite what the public is shown by mass media, teachers are not enslaved by their contractual obligations and many of these hard-working professionals go above and beyond what they're required to provide. It is the students who know how to speak to them and acknowledge them as professionals that will reap the benefits of teachers' altruism.

## Author's Findings

I conducted a study on high-achieving Black male students and their perceptions on the reasons for their high achievement and the reasons some Black male students were not achieving as high as they could be. For the purpose of this study high-achieving Black male students scored level 4 on both New York State Middle Level English language arts and mathematics assessments. When a student is said to achieve level 4, he or she has exceeded the proficiency standard. His or her performance demonstrates a thorough understanding of the English language arts or mathematics knowledge and skills expected at his/her grade level (NYSED, 2009). Out of a possible 262 Black male students attending the schools in the district where I conducted my study, only 10 met the selection criteria of scoring a level 4 on both assessments. If I were to study White male students, 45 would've met the selection criteria and there were fewer White male students in the grade levels I chose to study compared to

Black male students in these grades in this school district. This disparity is known as the Black-White test score gap and is part of a larger set of racial gaps that plague our country. These gaps exist in both urban and suburban areas and despite decades of research, discussions, and attempted solutions, these gaps remain.

## Author's Findings: Expectations

One of the high-achieving students in my study explained how some parents are not meeting their responsibilities and this led to lower achievement. He said,

> I think it's untrue you cannot be high achieving if you push yourself to [achieve] and your parents push you to [achieve]. If you're not high achieving sometimes it's the fault of the parents because they're not pushing you to be high achieving. If you are doing bad, they should tell you to go to extra help and to study more on the weekends and do better, and they keep encouraging you to stay in honors or in the classes you are in and not drop them. Because, mostly that parents don't influence them [lower-achieving male students] to do better and they choose not to do the work. Because if my parents didn't influence me, I wouldn't be in honors or AP or anything of the sort. I would be in Regents and doing the absolute minimum instead of doing the best that I can do.

This illustrates a tendency of too many parents allowing their children to decide what is best for them when typically children make decisions to reduce their effort. Honors and advanced placement work is more rigorous and more effectively prepares students for college. College admissions staff members will consider students who take Advanced Placement (AP) courses as being more likely to graduate from and add value to their institutions. If parents decide that their child will not enroll or remain in honors or Advanced Placement courses, they should require other activities that demand just as much effort and dedication. This is an example of setting a concrete expectation for high academic achievement and not allowing excessive amounts of leisure time. Another student described the ideal home for high-achieving students. He stated,

> It's not much fighting. There's definitely no physical violence. There is a good relationship between the- students, and their parents and that they can talk to their parents and their parents support them in school and encourage them to do well. Their parents are there, at their home. The children are not home by themselves and the parents spend time with them and, yeah that's pretty much it.

When asked why it was so important that parents be at home with their kids and that children were not home by themselves, he stated, "The parents act as role models for their children. They also act as guides in life so they seem [pause] like it's imperative that they're home to help their child."

## Author's Findings: School Performance Discussions

When asked if parents did not know when the report cards were to be mailed, this same student stated,

> They could either ask their sons or daughters or wait until the calendars that are given out.

Most children know that their parents should be aware when their report cards and progress reports will be distributed. Today's world is a place where that type of information is easily found on the Internet or from a phone call to the school or district office. When children see that their parents have not dedicated the effort needed to ensure they receive a report card or progress report soon after it has been distributed, they are communicating an abstract attitude about high academic achievement. The school staff also receives a message that the parent's talk is cheap and decides that this parent does not care about his/her child's education.

Two high-achieving males described how their parents kept continual communication lines open with their teachers about upcoming tests and quizzes. One student stated,

> I think first, the parent should ask their child. And if they feel compelled to go and set up a parent-teacher conference. If they [parents] feel that their child is doing well, and if the child tells them that they [*pause*] that he, was doing bad then they might want to talk to the teacher about it. But if the child feels and seems confident in what he or she is doing, and there doesn't really seem to be a problem then the parent can continue to wait and see if the problem goes away.

It was clear that the parents of these male students love their children. Ample praise was given when students shared exam grades they had received. When asked what would happen if any of these exam grades were lower than what they expected, parents indicated that they would engage the children in conversations about the amount of effort they had observed their sons put forth. These parents would ask their sons if they understood the material, and what actions would take place to ensure that either the material was better understood by the time the final examination would be given or how their sons were going to increase their effort. Negotiations regarding social activities that occurred during the weekend were regarded as the rewards that sons wanted and that parents were willing to offer. These young men may have wanted more material possessions than they had; however, they articulated that they did not need anything that they did not already have.

A second high-achieving student described the results of a conversation he had with his parents about lower than expected grades. He stated,

> There were times [*pause*], well I got grades on tests that I wasn't happy with. I knew that I had to pick it up or otherwise I'd get in trouble . . . I don't like getting yelled at by my parents because they can be kind of vicious but that's besides the point. [laughter] But yeah, things like not being able to hang out and no Xbox.

High-achieving students described the activities their parents participated in that supported their achievement in school. These activities ranged from supportive discussions that started out with "How are the test scores? Can I see an example of one of your tests? How do you feel about this class or how is this class going for you?" The first student described how his parents would help him if he sought their assistance,

> They will probably give me advice on how to do that. They would suggest certain things that I could do to improve my grades. Maybe they have their own method of studying that they remember. Maybe they know some,- maybe a community service option or an extracurricular sport that I can try. They would, if I asked them to, talk to my teacher, my guidance counselor. They would meet with me and discuss things I could do to bring up my grades.

Parents must make the time to support their children. The mother of one of the high-achieving students shared how her son was about to play an interscholastic soccer match. He was looking for her when she arrived a few minutes before the match began. Later, at home, he observed how tired his mother was, as she had many work responsibilities and was sleeping less in order to meet deadlines at work and carry out her home responsibilities. The son encouraged his mother not to attend the next game. The mother left her job, stating, "I realized that work was interfering with what I want to do for my children." Not all parents are in financial situations where they can leave a job; however, if parents are putting sleep, social activities, or community service before their children, then they are robbing their sons and daughters. Parents need to make choices to drive an ordinary car and spend some of that anticipated monthly luxury car note on cleaning services so they have more quality time to spend with their children. While the authors of this text advocate for assuming children's assigned chores occasionally to teach responsibility and negotiation, we do not believe that parents complete these chores before attending their child's music recital or basketball game, and definitely not before parents engage in those daily discussions about school and academic performance.

The majority of high-achieving males discussed how they negotiated with their parents to a point. Initially, one stated, "No, not really, no. I usually just go along with everything. I pick my battles [laughter]," when he described whether he negotiated with his parents. Later when asked to describe what he meant by "pick his battles," he stated, "Sometimes I get my way. When that does happen it's because I have to lay out the facts supporting my argument and then compare it to theirs as if I was debating." Another said that he "gets his way sometimes" and as he is getting older, he finds that happening "a little bit more now." Another high-achieving student described how his past performances on chores and school assignments helped him build a trusting relationship with his mother and allowed "one little thing [to] slip and still be okay." This relationship permitted him to negotiate the delay of completing his chores or the delay of his mother's disappointment if he did not complete an assignment on time. One of the mothers shared how she trusted her son's ability to negotiate with his teachers and his ability to improve his performance in the future so his final grade would not suffer as a result of seeing her son negotiate at home.

**Author's Findings: Inspect What You Expect**

Parents must develop relationships with their children so communication is honest and informs decisions. Teenagers will attempt to maximize the fun they think they are entitled to. Supervision of their leisure time is absolutely necessary until teenagers demonstrate they can be responsible with this precious commodity. The reason I choose to study high-achieving Black males was the opportunity for these males to discuss what they observed and heard regarding their male counterparts who were not achieving as well as they did. All of these successful students described parenting practices as a cause that resulted in lower achievement among other males who attended their schools. A high-achieving male described how parents who do not supervise their sons' academic progress adequately contributed to lower achievement. He said,

> There were a couple of people who are in my elective classes that try to keep their grades a secret. Like, they would hide the report cards and stuff like that but I wouldn't do that because if I'm in need of improvement, they [my parents] need to know. When the report cards are mailed and they [parents of lower achieving males] don't receive them at the right time they should ask about it and if not just call the school."

The first high-achieving student described his parents' support of his academic endeavors,

> Like, I am gonna say this from my point of view. My parents make sure that they are on top of me, to make sure that I am on top of everything. Like, they want to know when I have tests. Like, when I have quizzes, like, if I'm doing my homework. I think that an ideal parent of a good student is that they're going to be responsible and they're gonna

stay on top of their kid. It's like checking your
planner when you come home. By signing all the
tests and quizzes and even checking in with your
teacher at times, just to see how things are going.
My mom signs all the quizzes and tests and she
checks my planner every week, just to see what
was going on.

When asked how his mother knew about his academic progress
he stated, "She just asked me. Like, she'll ask when is the next
science test and I'll be like, we have one on Thursday or Friday."
The amount of parental control you exercise should be
related to the relationship that you have with your child and also
to their progress or attainment of their academic achievement
goals that you and your child have set. This is a very practical
and inexpensive reward. The first high-achieving student
described how his parents held him accountable for his academic
performance,

> They would, like, [*pause*] I'm not gonna say that
> they would take away everything that I have
> because they know that I'm working as hard as I
> can. Like I'm going to every extra help that I can
> to improve in that class. Then they're gonna try
> to help me too, instead of taking everything away
> and just lock me down. Like, this hasn't happened
> to me, but I would think that my parents would
> like, find a tutor or talk to the teacher to see if
> there's any, like, extra [*pause*] extra help that I
> can attend. Even if they [my parents] could help
> me with their own knowledge, they would do that.

This male's mother is a college graduate who worked part-time
supervised her children full-time, and maintained the household.
She described herself as being very active in the Parent Teacher
Association and the school district activities. One of the activities
that she discussed was her advocacy for her son. She stated, "My
knowledge of the schools and the staff members prevents my son

from being taken advantage of." Utilizing the data obtained, this mother is able to make decisions on the amount of advocacy at the school is needed, how much parental control needs to be applied, and when her son deserves a reward for his efforts and his results.

The parents of these high-achieving students indicated that their sons had household chore responsibilities. These responsibilities range from ensuring that younger siblings completed the homework before parents arrived home to the household maintenance task. These parents understood and communicated their understanding of the debate about students from low-income and working-class families having too much to do around the house and these responsibilities interfering with schoolwork. Each of these parents carefully considered the amount of work they asked their sons to complete as they reiterated that high academic achievement is their sons' top priority.

One high-achieving male had chores, which included other tasks besides keeping his bedroom clean, but he was able to negotiate not performing them regularly through demonstrated responsibility and forming a relationship with his mother that is filled with trust and openness. He said,

> There's like taking out the garbage, walking the dog, sometimes me and my sister do the dishes. My mom does the cleaning. She's a neat freak and then I have to clean my room, which I'm not good at. Like, my mom will tell me to take out the garbage and I'll be like "10 minutes" and then I'll end up forgetting. I think she knows me enough to know that I do most of my stuff that she tells me to do. What she tells me, but one little thing slips, it's like okay.

## Author's Findings: Support

Parental activities include family vacations and academic tutoring. One set of parents in my study described the importance of their family vacations. During these vacations, the family always included visits to local colleges and universities. Vacation time for this high-achieving student was also spent meeting and becoming acquainted with extended family members, especially those who have graduated from college. A cousin, who graduated from Columbia University and became an engineer, was discussed at length. His mother is a college graduate who supervises her three children and ensures the household is functioning. The father described himself as a gifted mathematics student who could not afford to complete his engineering degree. His son stated, "He is really good at math." The father's responsibilities included providing academic support to his son and his siblings in the areas of mathematics and science. His mother tutored her children in English and social studies. This high-achieving student said, "My mom would check my ELA essays because I wasn't good in seventh and eighth grade ELA. I'm pretty good now. She would proofread them." Every parent will not be able to assist their child by providing tutoring or be able to afford to travel out of the state or country for vacations; however, how limited time and money is invested in a child's future is where all parents can make a difference.

Another high-achieving student described the extracurricular support both his parents provide. He stated

> I play basketball for an out of school team and in the summer, I played baseball for an out of school team. My dad is the coach of the baseball team. And then for basketball, my mom and my dad are there on the sidelines. They are supporting me. My mom drives me. She is a taxicab. For baseball, it's my dad because my mom doesn't find it too interesting, so my dad drives me since he has to be there anyway. But for basketball, my mom usually comes out because she loves basketball.

While the high-achieving student's parents support their son's extracurricular activities and understand that their son's athletic prowess can help the chances of college and university admission and possibly scholarship money, the participation in these activities depended on the type of grades that their son brought home. When asked if they felt that they were overly controlling or too strict, these parents answered "no."

## How to Set High Concrete Academic Expectations

In my 3 decades of working with students and their parents, the commonality that each of the parents of the highly successful students had was their ability to set high academic expectations for their children's achievement. Presently, college admission is a must for all students. Some may argue that all children do not need to go, but the authors of this book argue that all children should have the choice to enroll in non-remedial college courses that are credit-bearing after they graduate from any United States high school. During a meeting with high school juniors at a large urban New York City high school, one student shared that he was not intending to go to college. He believed that his abilities were all physical. He has aspirations to become a professional boxer. He felt that his parents and older siblings, all of whom except his mother attended some college simply wanted to force their own plans for his life on to him. He also shared that he did not like the coursework and the effort that he had to expend in order to pass his Regents examinations and his classes. This young man was part of a group of students who were invited to participate in a college admissions mentoring program. At the time of our conversation, he had already passed two of the five New York State Regents examinations that he needed to graduate from his high school. His academic achievements allowed him to meet this meager criterion for placement in the group with the highest achievers; sadly, he is only one of the 50 male students out of a cohort of 200 males in this school to achieve this basic standard. At the time of my writing this chapter, I had not met his parents, but I applaud their efforts. The fact that their son could articulate his angst in the conversations that he was having with his family members about college indicated to me that this was a continual discussion. This story illustrates how frustrating it can be to have high expectations for your children, especially if they do not share them.

As parents, you must continue to have the highest expectations as you are modeling this behavior for children who will then learn to set high expectations for themselves. Too often children lower their prospects because they meet with difficulties and live in a society that bombards them with imagery that communicates they will not be successful if these expectations require high levels of academic achievement. Your children have earned the right to pursue their dreams and it starts with having an expectation they will achieve them.

As parents of secondary school students, it is a lot easier if you had these conversations when children were younger. However, you can still set high expectations but you do need to consistently communicate them and continually supervise your children's progress.

My father was not pleased with my high school grades but I could never understand why. I maintained a steady B average, and was attending one of the most selective public high schools in New York City. The children who lived in my public housing facility were not achieving the level of grades or attending the type of high school that I was. I felt my father's expectations were unfair. I didn't realize why I needed to have the 90s, 95's, and 100's that he was asking for. I didn't realize the types of grades that were necessary for me to gain acceptance at highly selective colleges and universities that I heard so much about from my father. Now I do.

Parents must show their children specific grades that are necessary to gain admission to the types of colleges they are expecting. "I want my child to go to college" is not good enough when a child is in the sixth grade. That statement, affirmation expectation has to be "I want my child to attend so-and-so college." When the conversation has that level of specificity then measurable achievement level goals can be set. The conversations that parents are having with their middle school child around specific colleges and universities now have grades that are attached to them.

There are sixth graders who state that they are going to go Harvard University. If your child is one of those students then as a parent, you should know the type of grades that Harvard University is expecting from the students they admit. When my father engaged in this conversation with me, there was no Internet. I was limited to my parents' social networks and the information they had. I was restricted to only the opportunities for poor Black male students that my parents and I knew about. Information is more accessible now.

Today's educational community recognizes the lack of knowledge that many parents of the soon to be first-generation college students have. I won't go as far as saying it is easy to gain this information so that you can convince your 10-year-old that they have to study harder and that the grades they are currently getting are not good enough; however, it is a lot easier than it was 10 or 20 years ago.

## How to Have School Performance Discussions

Parents do not have the luxury of being overly kind to our children. Lying to their children to save their self-esteem is not healthy behavior. All children must "confront the brutal facts of their current reality." Parents must allow them to deal with the truth but still come away from that encounter with their self-esteem intact. Many children attend high schools that do not offer the rigorous coursework that their peers are taking at higher performing high schools, yet everyone is competing for the same seats and scholarships. Since the coursework at different schools is not the same, colleges and universities have no choice but to consider the high school in which a child attends. If a child is in middle school at this time, there is no reason that he or she should not take the first year of high school mathematics and science before he or she moves up to the high school level. Until all assessments are designed in such a way that they do not give a clear advantage to children who enroll in high school course offerings in middle school and/or who begin to take college coursework in high school, parents have a responsibility to prepare their children for this competition. A child taking high school courses while in middle school and college courses while in high school is also taking advantage of a valuable opportunity to develop the skills that are necessary to deal with the rigor that he or she will encounter at the college and university level.

Parents of scholars talk about school daily. The conversation needs to include asking about friends, interactions that your son or daughter had during the course of the school day, and about what was learned. Parents who are beginning to have these conversations for the first time should not become discouraged if their child isn't a willing participant. Don't ask the questions that will allow the one-word answers that teenagers would like to give their parents. Nothing, Fine, or Okay (NFO) responses are not going to give parents the data that they need to determine the correct course of action for their children and for themselves. Parents should be having conversations about results from examinations that their child has on a weekly basis.

The longest that I've seen good teachers go without providing some sort of assessment of learning to their students has been 2 weeks. We must ask our children about quiz results and the return of any tests, projects, or papers on a weekly basis. We must ask specifically about subjects, particularly the ones where our child has not achieved the specific grade goal that we have set. If 3 weeks of school goes by without our child reporting specific results on assessment from any class, we should call the school and leave a message for our child's teacher. We should expect a return phone call no later than 48 hours from the day that we left a message. It is important that we keep track of these details using a calendar planner or a "To Do" list application. There are several good apps that will help us manage this on our smart phones.

Helping your child become a scholar is one of the most important jobs that you will ever undertake in your life. It is important that you have all the resources that you need to complete this job to the best of your ability. If the teacher does not get back to you within the 48-hour timeframe than it's time for you to speak with that teacher's department supervisor or the school administrator. You are all very busy people; however, your child's education is your top priority. It is important that you advocate for your child and getting the right data is a step in the correct direction.

It is important that you praise your children when they've achieved their goals. Praise and reward help to build and sustain your son's or daughter's motivation to achieve academically. Eventually, you're hoping that this motivation to achieve will come from your son or daughter. In the meanwhile, you must provide rewards such as praise or less parental control when your children have earned them. Praise is free and will teach your child that you are ever-vigilant in their pursuit of academic excellence. Rewards do not have to be expensive. Allowing your child to stay at a friend's house for an extra half hour or to allow your child's friends to come over and stay the night are excellent rewards for achieving academically. Cooking or purchasing your child's favorite meal because they've earned it by achieving or showing progress toward a stated goal is another effective reward. Allocating free time to do what your child wants to, which may mean sacrificing some sleep on your part, is also an excellent reward. You will need to spend time building a relationship if the communication about academics is going to be open and honest. When you have open communication with your son or daughter, the amount of time that you have to spend interacting with school staff to obtain the data on your child's performance becomes less.

Not every exam, grade, long-term paper or project will result in the type of grades that both you and your child expect. When this happens it is important that you continue to praise your child for the effort that they are expending and identify subjects that your child can spend more time studying. There is no substitute for quality study time. If your child is to become a scholar, an identity that will last a lifetime, you will have to teach them the importance of hard work and time management.

## How to Inspect What You Expect

As parents, we must develop a plan with our children to achieve their life goal. Helping children to identify these goals and starting with the end outcome in mind is something that the wealthy have always done. During one of my presentations to high school seniors on developing concrete expectations and a college admissions plan, I shared that my research found that many students begin this process in the 6th grade. A guidance counselor came over and praised my presentation but he informed me that the parents of wealthy children begin this type of planning once their child is born. Plans are like anything else that can change, they should be fluid. It is fine to change our plan if it is not helping meet the goals we have set. This is a lesson that we must teach our children early. Middle and high school students setting goals for high school or college admission are great practice for when our children plan their career goals. In this new economy that we are living in, mistakes made along the career trajectory are graver than they were decades ago. When I graduated with an industrial engineering degree and a 2.6 GPA it was very easy for me to find a job. Now, for every job, there are 10 to 15 highly qualified applicants.

There is a philosophy that it is better to create a job then to apply for one. Creating a job requires setting concrete expectations, developing a plan, and gaining valuable experience while in college. If this is what you aspire for your children than you have a responsibility to teach them how to plan and measure their progress toward their goals. But like any good plan, it is only as good as the data and information that you have researched to inform the planning process. This is why it is important for you and your child to conduct research on high schools, colleges, and careers. There are simply not enough mentors and guidance counselors for your child to receive the personalized attention that he or she deserves when coming to this very critical planning process, unless you are willing to pay for it.

Once a specific grade criterion is set for each course your son or daughter is taking, you must ensure that you meet with your child to review their progress toward each objective. Conversations with teachers must be shared with your child. Reviewing progress reports, report cards, returned tests homework, papers, projects, or anything else that has been reviewed by the teacher together are mandatory tasks that you and your child must complete. Some educators call this process "data chats." Schools should conduct data chats with your child frequently. Depending on the type of school your child attends these data chats will or will not occur. As a parent, you have a right to ensure that these data chats are occurring; however, you must not replace advocacy for your parental responsibility to engage your child in these data chats. You should engage in both. During these data chats, you must identify the progress measure you will discuss. For example, a recently returned math test should be discussed in the context of the learning goal for mathematics. The discussion of this mathematics test score and how it is either good enough or needs to be improved is related to the final grade in mathematics that your child is working toward. This conversation on the final grade in mathematics relates to the successful attainment of a final grade in the next mathematics course and how this grade looks on your child's transcript. The transcript grade relates to a conversation on admission to the high school or college of choice. These repeated conversations may seem boring and redundant but they are necessary to reinforce your expectations with your son or daughter.

The relationship that we have with our sons or daughters reflects the trust and honesty that we have been building throughout the years when our children volunteers the grades that we need to see. I have met too many parents who believe that this relationship is a sign of weakness on the part of their child, and that only the "goody-goody" students engage in this behavior. Well, our children need to be "goody-goody," if that's what it takes to meet their academic achievement goals. If our children cannot share a test grade with us, how do we expect them to share the more important decisions that they need to make and not lie to us? As parents of teenage children, we begin to see the transition from authoritative parent to one who is a friend and mentor. Our life experiences are always something of great value and who better to share this treasure with than our own sons or daughters. If we go back to our conversation on expectations, the sharing of the grades is a non-negotiable expectation we must have. Children who hide report cards and progress reports from their parents are walking down a road that will eventually lead them to places we don't want them to be.

Anytime our children engage in such deceit, we must take a stand and not tolerate this behavior. The first step in teaching our children our expectation that all their grades and returned work is to be shared, is demonstrating our knowledge of when reports of our children's progress will be distributed by the school.

During open school nights, parent-teacher conferences back-to-school nights, or any other curriculum event when you have an opportunity to meet your child's teachers, you should find out the frequency in which your child's instructor assigns assessments. You should also find out what the teacher's policy is on returning assessments to children and what system is in place for communicating the actual test grades that your child has earned. Do not allow your child's teachers to interpret whether or not your child is meeting your expectations. There are many great educators who have the highest set of standards for the children that they teach, but there are also too many that have a low set of standards. You eliminate the possibility of your child attaining a standard that is way too low for their long-term goals by communicating the expectation you have to both your child and to their teachers. When teachers understand that you have an expectation for certain grades and that you continually review the progress that your child is making, the teachers will become more supportive of your efforts in developing a scholar.

As discussed earlier, the assignment of chores requires a delicate balance between responsibility and academic achievement expectation. You should assign your child chores as they need to know that there's a price that must be paid for anything of value. The type of chore really doesn't matter. Children must be taught responsibility and that with effort comes some sort of compensation. Children who are given everything without having to earn anything end up being life-long children. Chores are easy ways to monitor children's work ethic. Chores should not take more than a half hour per day and can last longer on the weekends. Chores should not consume so much time that children cannot participate in extracurricular activities or develop meaningful social relationships with their peers. Becoming a scholar is also becoming a leader. The ability to motivate other human beings to act in the best interests of an organization is a skill that is more valuable than anything else children will learn. One hundred people can produce so much more than one person. That is why the supervisor of 100 people will receive more compensation than any of the hundred he or she supervises (professional athletics may be one of the few exceptions). The assignment of chores should not prevent children from learning the social skills necessary to motivate others.

The assignment of chores must not end with the parent doing the chore for his or her child without proper negotiation. This means that parents can loan their children time in order for their children to complete an assignment that is due or to study just a little bit more for an upcoming test. Children need to pay their parents back by doing extra chores when their schedules permit. Allow children to negotiate delaying the completion of chores or having someone else complete a chore for later consideration. The ability to negotiate with teachers is an important skill for scholar. Children develop this skill by negotiating with parents.

## Types of Support Parents Must Provide

Having two parents in the household is definitely an advantage. I admire single mothers who are able to engage in the following parental activities without aid from the man who helped create their son or daughter. Single parents need a support network that allows them to engage in these activities and assist them in raising their scholar. These activities include:

1. Providing transportation to allow our children to participate in extra help sessions, community-based mentoring programs, extracurricular activities, and cultural events.

2. Providing support in the form of tutoring or supplemental instruction. Many of us become intimidated by the edu-speak that the teachers and administrators engage in. Our sons and daughters need basic literacy, writing, and

mathematic skills in order to successfully master more difficult coursework. Our children are never too old to have us as parents act as a peer proofreader of their writing.

3. Attending our daughter' or son's extracurricular activities including practices or rehearsals but especially athletic contests, performances, or academic showcases. We are trying to build a relationship of trust with our daughters and sons. This relationship is strengthened when they see our sacrifice of time to support the activities that are important to them. To compete at the secondary level interscholastic athletic competition, or to perform in a play or concert, or to have the honor of having work showcased at school, required a great deal of effort and sacrifice on the part of our children. They deserve our time. Our attendance is a necessary and enjoyable part of being a parent and shows our children that we love and support them.

4. Advocating for our children's education. The parents of scholars access a social network to learn who are the best teachers and tutors that their children can have. Not everyone can access a social network possessing this information. We as parents have a responsibility to advocate for our sons' or daughters' best interests with middle or high school teachers and administrators. Advocacy is not the loud screaming that occurs too often in our schools. Teachers and administrators are hard-working professionals that have the responsibility to develop our sons and daughters into individuals that become productive citizens. As parents, we must recognize this and remain respectful despite the frustration of not having our children meet their goals or show progress toward them. Respectful communication does not mean that we fail to obtain what our children need from the school. Being consistent and determined in the face of adversity is the responsibility that we have

when advocating for our children. It may take a little longer for us to obtain what we need for our children but we must remain steadfast.

5.  Discussing future aspirations of your children. It is acceptable for our teenage children not to know how they want to make money when they are older. It is unacceptable for our teenagers to be unable to articulate the type of lifestyle they want to have when they become adults. By discussing lifestyle (type of house, type of car, type of neighborhood that they want to live in, what they will enjoy doing with the money that they earn) we are having the beginning conversations that we must have with our children so they can begin to explore careers.

6.  Visiting colleges and universities will make the specific grades that we set with our sons or daughters more meaningful. When our sons or daughters hear from the college admissions staff members what type of grades that they need for admission, the specific goals are no longer just mommy or daddy talking. I was one of those children that had to find out information for myself. The discovery of something new was always and continues to be a joy for me. There are many children who are like me and need to hear firsthand from someone who is in a position that they aspire to be. Spending the time with our children to visit these places and meet these people are wonderful opportunities to improve our relationships with our children but also gather the data that we need to develop our children's college admission plan.

7.  Providing boundaries on non-academic time activities. Our children cannot always make the best decisions for themselves due to their lack of experience. It is important that we establish boundaries on the amount of leisure time that our children have and where they spend this leisure time. We must know our child's friends and their parents. Arranging times to meet with the parents of the children that our sons or daughters are spending time

with is not something that could be done; it must be done! Our children who have not met their academic goals and are not attaining the specific grades that have been set cannot have large amounts of time to play video games, watch TV, and surf on the Internet. Just like a child who will only eat desserts if allowed to, our children will pick leisure activities before additional academic ones if they are not molded into scholars.

## Conclusion

I began this chapter by mentioning a study that was conducted in Finland. Children from other countries understand at a much earlier age when compared to American children, what a better life looks, feels, and sounds like. Fortunately our children in the United States are not always dealing with civil wars, the denial of human rights, and other atrocities that too many children elsewhere are more familiar with. Our children have the time and freedom to pursue high levels of academic achievement. We have a responsibility to our children to continually orient them toward their future. These conversations about our children's future need to move from the abstract to the concrete by developing action plans and trajectories toward goals once we developed them. This is a continual process and these conversations are continually revisited well beyond the high school years. Many of our children attending middle and high school have no idea of what is beyond their own communities. Visiting different parts of the country and the higher education institutions there, in addition to facilitating conversations between our children and professionals, are two activities that we must do with our children if we hope to raise scholars. A child who states that they want to become a doctor but never had a conversation with one to find out how he or she became a doctor is a person who is still demonstrating abstract expectations. Who is responsible for those missed opportunities? As parents we are responsible for moving our children from the abstract to the concrete world of planning. This requires that we utilize our social networks to the benefit of our children. Through our social networking, we will be able to identify a professional that may have a life altering conversation with our sons or daughters. These are conversations we must have if we are truly preparing our children for college and not prison walls.

# Chapter 5:
# Practices for Incarcerated Parents That Lead to High Academic Achievement

# Dr. Michelle Gantt

Compared to the prison populations throughout the world the United States of America has the highest rate of incarceration. There are 2.3 million Americans behind bars. One in 87 working-aged White men is in prison or jail compared with 1 in 36 Hispanic men and 1 in 12 Black men. These prison walls have detained over 800,000 parents, which have ultimately affected the lives of over two million children. The actual number of families that have experienced incarceration is unknown. Given unprecedented growth in prison populations, it is remarkable that so little attention has been given in social science literature to the experiences of families impacted by incarceration (Arditti, Smock, & Parkman, 2005).

Many children with an incarcerated parent are students in our nation's classrooms. This unique group of children is truly a forgotten group. Recognizing the role of an incarcerated parent and the impact of imprisonment on children is imperative to a child's academic success. Ultimately, educational institutions and families who have experienced incarceration would achieve higher levels of success by providing support services and collaborating with this unique group of children and their families.

Being sentenced to prison should not remove you from your role as a parent or take away your rights. Your parental status is not a contributing factor in the justice system when you are convicted of a crime. However, the children are the unseen victims of the parent's prison sentence. Prison separates people from their families and community. Due to the restrictions placed on inmates through criminal justice policies and procedures parenting from prison is even more challenging. A parent who is at home raising their children could never imagine the difficulty.

Many parents' are being sentenced to months, years, or sometimes life in prison. While incarcerated, these parents must learn to understand the written and unwritten rules of prison life. Some of the life changing issues they may also face include fear of harm, shame, hate, anxiety, and a deep sense of loss. In addition to their adjustment to prison they must continue their dual roles as inmate, parent, spouse, sibling, and friend.

Parenting while incarcerated will have an impact on the entire family unit. Maintaining contact with loved ones during incarceration is impacted by costs and time restraints. The telephone and mail are the most common methods used by parents in prison to communicate. Parents can talk with their families for a predetermined amount of time and price. Issues may arise that will also restrict the use of the telephone (institutional lockdowns or disciplinary sanctions). Incarcerated parents in many cases are housed two to eight hours away from their family residence. Their facility designation is based on numerous factors, such as level of offense or criminal history. Therefore, the family will incur the inconveniences as well as the costs associated with traveling (lodging, food, fuel, etc.).

Prior to visiting an imprisoned parent, the child and caregiver may be required to submit their personal information for a criminal background check as well as a search of their bodies via metal detector machines and/or handheld metal detectors. The family members may also be screened for the use of narcotics. In some cases they are required to wait outside on lines in unfavorable weather conditions. The family must be familiar with the visiting policies, procedures, schedules, and the dress code or it will affect their ability to be approved for a visit.

Depending on the type of correctional institution contact with the parent can be extremely limited. During visitation prisons have rules for how and when parents can hug, kiss, or show any type of affection to their children. Incarcerated parents may be confined to designated areas which are usually defined by colored lines indicating where they are permitted to move around. Unfortunately, in some high security cases parents and children may have no contact and are separated by a glass window during visitation. Also, the incarcerated parents and the family members are monitored by prison personnel and video cameras in the visiting areas.

Considering the limitations due to policies and procedures, parenting from prison can be difficult. However family disruption connected to the incarceration of a parent is a minimally explored area of research. Once a parent is incarcerated the dynamics of the family is significantly impacted. The children will now be raised in a single family household with other family members, or in some cases in a foster home. Many families will experience a significant decline in their financial and social status. Ultimately, everyone may face high levels of psychological and emotional distress.

Regardless of a parent's financial contribution or level of involvement, he or she has a significant influence on his or her children's lives. Incarcerated parents want to have key roles in fostering their children well-being. These parents have the same dreams, goals, and aspirations for their children. Many of them have a deep desire to have a positive relationship with their children. The majority of the parents in prison state their crimes were a result of trying to provide for their family.

In addition to their current situation many incarcerated parents have limited parenting skills and others may not know how to actively parent from prison to maintain a positive relationship with their child. As most parents do they want to positively contribute to their children's lives. For many of these parents their incarceration has heightened their need to understand the importance of communication, quality time, and the need to establish or maintain a meaningful relationship with their children. Family relationships are their greatest connection to the outside world. They are no longer in control of making the decision of when they are going to see, hear, or touch their child. As many parents question their influence on their child's life incarcerated parents live with uncertainty daily. The type of questions these parents ask may include: How will I explain my incarceration? How can I prevent my children from being incarcerated? How can I still be a parent and raise my children from a prison? Will my children be safe? Will my children still love me? Who will take care of my children?

Having an incarcerated loved one places a strain on family relationships emotionally, financially, and socially. Inmates are stigmatized, criticized, ridiculed, and looked down upon by society for having been imprisoned. Incarceration places a heavy burden on the family unit and can have an emotional and psychological impact on the lives of children especially.

The incarceration of a parent affects the child as well as the parent's ability to be a parent during incarceration. Issues a parent in prison may encounter are revealed through the voices of some incarcerated parents in a federal facility:

*My 19-year-old daughter called me "selfish." She asked me how could you get locked up again? How could you not care about us? I explained to her that while I may have been wrong, I did what I thought was right. Now I realize parenthood is more than buying a gift or going to restaurants, it is the sharing of quality time.*

*It is challenging to learn how to be a parent in here. We should not be discouraged by the rules and regulations of this institution. We should not stop trying to help other families in this situation. There is no safe space on the unit to talk about your kids. Everyone is worried or bragging about everything else.*

*I'm going to miss their birthday parties and graduations.*

*I'm not sure if my children are being treated right. I think my family just wants them for the money.*

## Children of Incarcerated Parents

The effects of incarceration on a child in many cases are unknown or not addressed by the judicial system, the community, and the school system or family members. Some children feel like they are doing time with their parents. The same fear of harm, shame, hate, and a deep sense of loss is felt by both the parent and the child. This is truly a special group of children who do not receive enough attention, guidance, or consideration.

These children are the unseen, unconsidered result of a crime and a prison sentence. Some children have witnessed the arrest of their parents or have watched them being actively involved in criminal activity (selling or using drugs, fighting, stealing, prostituting, carrying illegal firearms, etc.). There are families with multiple generations (grandparents, parents, and siblings) who are incarcerated. Some of the children in these families are being raised in courtrooms and prison visiting rooms.

The effects of separation on the children of incarcerated parents can be significant. In 1992, Gabel's study with incarcerated children found that 92% of the children with an incarcerated father in the United States missed the affection he provided and 59% of the children felt lonely. Many children have experienced the trauma of sudden separation from their sole caregiver. As a result, most of them were vulnerable to feelings of anxiety, anger, sadness, depression, and guilt.

Many children feel like they do not have anyone to share their feelings with concerning their parent's incarceration. Family members are sometimes not an option because they are unsure of how to handle the separation and are in pain themselves. These children are also in fear of being ridiculed or ostracized. Many of them question the type of relationship they will have with their imprisoned parent. The parents and the children live with uncertainty and fear of their future as a family. The type of questions these children may ask include: How will I explain why my parent is incarcerated? How can I prevent myself from being incarcerated in the future? How can my mom or dad raise me from prison? Who will protect me and take care of me? Will my mom or dad still love me? Why did this happen to me?

With all these questions and concerns these children may have felt deception, guilt, or anger regarding their parent's incarceration because they feel like their parent was taken away from them. There are times when they take the blame for their parents being in prison. Living under abnormal conditions they are stuck with the pressures of continuing life as a normal child. Children of incarcerated parents face a higher risk of experiencing poverty as well as social and emotional issues (Parke & Clarke-Stewart, 2002). They may express themselves by exhibiting aggression and other negative behaviors.

Not only is the incarcerated parent's role impacted, the role of the child will also be affected. In some families the child now has to play a more significant role. For example, they may have to take on more of a leadership role to their younger siblings. The male child will have to take on the role of protector to keep the family safe. The female child may take on more chores by cooking and cleaning. In order to help provide basic necessities for the family, these children are worried about finding ways to help with the household expenses and daily operations. School is usually at the bottom of the list of concerns for children experiencing parental incarceration.

Some younger children with an imprisoned parent may experience developmental issues and learning problems (Magaletta & Herbst, 2001; Parke & Clarke-Stewart, 2002). The possibilities of these children experiencing behavioral problems are significant. The absence of positive intervention along with emotional withdrawal, failure in school, and delinquency were a few negative outcomes the child of a parent in prison encountered (Seymour, 1998). As children reach adolescence, suspension and drop-out rates are higher for these children (Trice & Brewster, 2004).

In many cases the break down in the family unit and changes in roles and responsibilities affect the child's ability to focus on their role as a student. As a result, there may be no time or interest in the completion or accuracy of homework, school projects, or events. The caregiver may not have the time or knowledge to recognize their important role as educators in the child's life. So now there may be an absence of a positive role model to give the child support, be an example of educational excellence, and exert positive discipline techniques or to just spend meaningful quality time.

Many of these children spend several years being impacted by their parent's' incarceration, sometimes 5–10 years. Others become adults during their parent's imprisonment; sentences may range from 10 years to life in prison. Many are scarred permanently by their parent's incarceration. Children of incarcerated parents were three to six times more likely to exhibit violent or serious delinquent behavior (Eddy & Reid, 2002). The behavior problems that started as a child could be linked to a family history of legal problems, irresponsible behaviors, and parents with poor disciplinary skills (Eddy & Reid, 2002). These children are at a high risk for intergenerational incarceration.

The effects of incarceration on the parent and the child are revealed through voices of incarcerated parents. The issues highlighted in research are validated from some incarcerated parents of a federal facility:

*How do we fix the damage to our children? My 11-year-old is accused of having a mental disorder because of her pain in dealing with my incarceration. Programs need to focus on damage to the children.*

*Before I could only see my children every 3 or 4 months. Now I have an opportunity to see them once a month. Children see us so incapacitated in jail; they see our restrictions and suffering.*

*How do you do time as a parent with a sentence of over 10 years? How do you teach children how to deal with the time?*

*Are there things a parent should look out for? My children told me that they have put their lives "on hold" while I am in here. We are still a parent even while we are in here. I have not seen them since I have been incarcerated.*

## Educational Institutions

There are laws involving the education of children with an incarcerated parent. Thus far these laws focus on the areas concerning children with special education needs and foster care placements. New York State Education Law Section 3212 addresses imprisoned and/or parents confined to a prison. Legally, a parent is "imprisoned" when he or she has pled guilty to or been convicted of a crime and is serving time, sanctioned by a judge in a correctional facility. If the parent is incarcerated but has not yet been sentenced and is awaiting trial, or the trial is in progress, the local Department of Education must contact the parent to inform them of issues involving the child's educational status or concerns.

When a child is in foster care and their parent is imprisoned, parental rights are still recognized. The parent retains the authority to make education decisions about his or her child. This law requires educational personnel to communicate with the imprisoned parent unless the parent's rights have been terminated or surrendered. When a child is not in foster care and is living with someone else because the birth or adoptive parent is imprisoned, the local Department of Education is not required to contact the parent (Advocates for Children of New York 2010).

According to the Family Educational Rights and Privacy Act (FERPA) all parents can access their child's school records unless a court order or other legal document specifically revokes these rights. In New York City, all non-custodial parents including incarcerated parents have the right to review their child's educational records unless a judge has ruled otherwise. Schools can mail the student's records to the parent (Advocates for Children of New York, 2010).

Many educational institutions have not created specific plans to involve incarcerated parents in the decision making concerning their child's special education concerns. In most cases, the rights of parents in prison are not explored or considered. Educational systems rarely, if ever have mentioned or researched the family disruption connected to the incarceration of a parent or its negative impact on the academic or behavioral success of a child. When children experience divorce, death, or abuse their opportunity to be referred for counseling can be immediate. Many school personnel do not recognize, understand, or are unfamiliar with the effects of parental incarceration. Therefore, when a parent is incarcerated referring that student for counseling may not be considered or it may be delayed.

There are many factors that affect the schools' ability to address the needs of children experiencing parental incarceration. Some families are unfamiliar with the effects of parental incarceration on the children's lives until issues arise. Many times family members are unwilling to share this information with school personnel. Parents may feel like the schools are not concerned with this issue or they may not know who can address it. The parents may also be afraid of being ridiculed or ostracized.

There are schools located in areas that are significantly impacted by parental and intergenerational incarceration. Our nation's prisons continue to lead with the number of incarcerated parents and the number of children being impacted by incarceration in comparison to other countries. Incarceration affects everyone. It is not gender, race, or socioeconomic specific. These special students are sitting in classrooms with little to no services or support.

Below are two statements from an administrator sharing their need to understand the effects of incarceration on their students.

> *I have a troubled student in school with a father that was always in and out of prison. I never considered how his parent's' incarceration could affect him, until I read your dissertation.*

*In this area there are so many children suffering from generations in prison, where do we begin? How do we help these children?*

## Suggestions for Raising Scholars with an Incarcerated Parent

As a correctional worker in a federal prison I hear the concerns and fears of incarcerated parents on a continuous basis. In addition to my professional experience, my educational and personal experiences contribute to my knowledge and ability to provide a framework or plan to increase the chances for a successful life for children that have experienced parental incarceration. All parties involved must collaborate to promote the awareness of the effects of parental incarceration and to create programs and services for these families. Ultimately parents and/or caregivers must inform and involve educational personnel in matters concerning parental incarceration. Furthermore, the parents' that participate in parenting programs significantly increases their opportunity to positively influence their child's life as well as the relationships within the family. The support and positive interaction amongst the family will reduce the chances of the parent returning to prison and/or intergenerational incarceration. With access to appropriate resources, support services and the implementation of the strategies presented in this book, families experiencing incarceration can demolish the stigmas and negative statics associated with having a parent in prison; thus allowing the parents to focus on the skills needed to raise their children to become scholars.

The following recommendations are the results of my experiences and research. The research-based parenting program "The Role of a Father" provides incarcerated parents with strategies to address the specific challenges incarcerated parents may face while in prison. Parents in prison will identify strategies to help them to contribute to their child's chances to become successful scholars. Additionally, the custodial parent and/or caregiver raising the child in the home will need to identify strategies to obtain support from school personnel and community organizations to assist them with raising their children to become scholars.

## The Incarcerated Parent

Incarcerated parents must understand the structural barriers (communication, prison regulations, financial burdens family support) they may encounter while parenting from prison. Identifying these barriers will help them to continue to actively parent from prison. In order for incarcerated parents to remain engaged and actively involved while in prison they must persistently identify strategies to maintain a parent-child relationship despite the prison's procedural and structural barriers.

In addition to the numerous issues parents in prison face they can and must be supported and encouraged to continue to fulfill their parenting role. Understanding the unique challenges imprisonment places on parents may hinder them from executing all of the traditional parental roles. However, the maintenance of parent-child bonds can and should be promoted during incarceration. Parents in prison should also continue to be involved in decisions concerning their child's daily activities and educational progress. Furthermore, these parents must identify the most effective way to exemplify educational excellence discipline, respect, and positive and meaningful communication as well as the importance of having a high level of self-esteem and emotional and social well-being.

A lack of education may have limited incarcerated parents ability to effectively provide their children with tools to become successful students (Beckert, Strom, & Strom, 2007). In this case, it is important for parents in prison to understand their role as an educator in their children's lives. These parents must be seen as a role model for education. Parental education is an important predictor of child achievement. Having incarcerated parents enhance their vocational and educational levels will also provide them with knowledge to interact with their children differently.

Sample strategies and activities for parents in prison to raise scholarly children are:

- Inform the child, custodial parent/caregiver and school staff of your desire to be actively involved in your child's education
- Request copies of school calendars, records special events and report cards
- Identify the best communication method between you and the school
- Schedule teleconferences for educational updates with the school (Providing the imprisoned parent with information concerning assignments or behavioral progress reports will help the child and the incarcerated parent feel like they are being supported and are receiving tools to succeed despite this challenging situation)
- Consistently communicate your educational expectations with your child
- Assist your child with school projects by researching information in the prison library or obtain information from educational staff and/or inmates
- Participate in a parenting program to identify activities to enhance your role as parent
- Increase your educational levels by participating in programs on site or through distance learning programs.

Children's cognitive development is influenced by the parent's' level of education. Research studies have found the influence of a parent's education significantly correlates with the measures of children's functions such as problem solving planning, and strategy development (Ardila, Rosselli, Matut, & Guajardo, 2005). In addition, children with highly educated parents also have a larger vocabulary, more rapid language development, better performance in cognitive tests, and higher school attendance (Hoff-Ginsberg, 1991).

The imprisoned parent and the custodial parent and/or caregiver are responsible for the foundation and motivation for their child's ability to become scholars despite the negative effects of parental incarceration. Sample strategies and activities for custodial parents to raise scholarly children are:

- Participate in adult educational and parenting programs
- Obtain support from school personnel and community organizations
- Request support services from the guidance counselor
- Educate the school's personnel on the effects of parental incarceration on children
- Inform your child's teacher and principal of the parent's imprisonment
- Stay actively involved in your child's education and share your academic expectations
- Identify and participate in the school's programs and community programs
- Include the imprisoned parent in decisions pertaining to the child's education.

It is important for families experiencing incarceration to inform school personnel of the types of stressors these students may encounter compared to traditional students. Some of the students with an incarcerated parent may not look forward to celebrating birthdays, Father's Day or Mother's Day, and/or any other significant holiday. Custodial parents should provide information for the staff to understand their child's needs and challenges. Additionally, they should identify literature and relevant community resources for the school's personnel to increase their awareness and understanding of parental incarceration.

Activities the custodial and imprisoned parent can suggest for schools to increase the academic success for students experiencing parental incarceration include:

- Partnering with community organizations that provide services to children with a parent in prison to increase the school's understanding of this population
- Identifying professional seminars that focus on the effects of parental incarceration for counselors and educators to participate in, which will afford them the opportunity to create appropriate programs and services to address the children's emotional, social, and educational concerns
- Initiating support services that include peer groups for parents facing the fears of incarceration
- Post signs and email facts informing all stakeholders within the school system of the effects of incarceration and the schools desire to help and enhance the lives of this special group. The stigma associated with incarcerated individuals would be reduced by engaging the caregivers of the students in school activities and events as well
- Implement a parenting program for all parents with additional services for parents experiencing parental incarceration.

To increase their child's academic success the custodial and imprisoned parent must ensure that family members and school personnel perform the following:

- Provide emotional and academic support
- Encourage the child to communicate their feelings concerning the parent's incarceration and the child's abilities as a student
- Identify additional educational services for the child to receive that addresses areas of concern in the school and the community

- Ask the child to keep both parents informed of grades, projects, and school events
- Motivate the child to continuously participate in school counseling and extracurricular activities.

Having these children feel connected to adults and children in the school that understand their situation without judgment or prejudice may improve the student's' academic, behavioral, and social-emotional levels (Johnson, 2006). This support may encourage them to participate in school activities and to positively address their concerns and fears associated with their parents' incarceration. These students will become empowered through positive social networking. Also, encouraging them to participate in community group projects and team sports or clubs will help them to establish positive relationships with their peers and to find support within these groups from other caring adults and professionals. These types of interactions would significantly help to reduce the pain of being lonely and feeling forgotten and misunderstood.

It is also important for the parents to identify community organizations to partner with to provide consistency and structure between home and school. Having the student involved in afterschool programs and community programs will increase his or her chances of formulating positive relationships to aid in the increase of their academic, behavioral, and social success.

**Parenting Programs**

Participating in parenting programs will help both the custodial parent and the incarcerated parent attain and/or increase their parenting techniques and knowledge of their role. These parents need to enroll in a program that provides information to help parents in prison to develop positive relationships with their spouses and children, identify family values, and to develop or enhance their role as educational role models. Programs that include the elements listed above would positively enhance the parent-child relationship as well as the student's academic success.

The study conducted by Thombre, Montague, Maher, and Zohra (2009) revealed incarcerated parents believed addressing communication and education issues for their children was needed for their children to avoid imprisonment and to increase the child's chances for a more successful life. Parenting programs have suggested that the more involved incarcerated parents were and the more attached to their children they were resulted in lower levels of intergenerational crime (Bushfield, 2004; Restrepo, 2007). Furthermore, improving the relationship between children and their incarcerated parent, when it was in the best interest of the child, was vital to preventing intergenerational criminality (Covington, 1995).

It is time for incarcerated parents to get educated prepared, and excited about parenting. It is imperative that they understand how every interaction and reaction they have will impact their child's life, forever and in various ways. It will not only enhance their relationship as a family, it may prevent them from being incarcerated as a juvenile or an adult. Research shows children of incarcerated parents are five times more likely to become incarcerated (Wakefield, 2007).

It would be beneficial for incarcerated parents to be involved in a parenting program that will identify strategies to help them to continue to actively parent despite their individual barriers. The program must also provide an understanding of the impact of prison on the children and the family unit. It is imperative for these programs to provide parents in prison with activities to counteract negative family consequences resulting from his or her incarceration.

The type of contact an incarcerated parent and their child have during incarceration will significantly impact their relationship during incarceration and beyond. Parents in prison and the custodial parents must identify supportive services that are initiated during incarceration and during the re-entry phase. Affording inmates opportunities to maintain positive and sustaining contacts with their families improves the chances of a successful reintegration with their role as a parent and contributing member of society.

## Sample Parenting Practices

In 2010 my research defined parenting practices as behaviors that could affect parent-child relationships and interactions. It included parenting practices as caretaking and shared activities. The practices emphasized the need for parents to focus on appropriate discipline and communication strategies it also focused on how parents instill respectful behaviors in children as well as a financial education.

The custodial parent and the imprisoned parent can positively impact their relationship as a family and increase their child's ability to become a scholar by participating in a program that incorporates topics such as communication, discipline respect, and different types of parent-child interactions. The programs these parents participate in will need to encourage direct contact between the incarcerated parent and the child to increase shared activities, decision-making, and relationship building. It will need to incorporate creative and unconventional strategies and practices to help custodial parents and incarcerated parents to identify ways to continue to actively parent while confined in prison. It is also important to create an environment that encourages families with an imprisoned parent to share their feelings and to discuss their successful parenting strategies and challenges. The methods used to communicate must be supportive, honest, critical, and positive between the parents and children. Communication is a critical area that also needs to include discussions concerning, sex, negative behaviors, and other conflicts. Discussions between the custodial parent incarcerated parent, and the child may encourage everyone to share their need to feel and show love, reveal the pain and discomfort of the separation and their expectations and fears regarding the health and well-being of the family.

The parental training provided must include activities to enhance the types of interactions incarcerated parents will have with their child while they are imprisoned. Sample activities include writing wish lists (identify and share their wishes as a family), feeling letters (identify and share activities expressing how their emotions are affected by various situations), sending and receiving puzzles to complete together via mail, as well as jokes, quotes, and facts. The parents and the child must be encouraged to actively communicate.

In the quotes below incarcerated parents shared their views on the positive impact of participating in a parenting program:

*We should all encourage others to participate to learn how to talk with their children while incarcerated.*

*Communication helped me to overcome my fear to address issues that I thought might rub salt in a wound.*

*Some of the techniques afforded me the opportunity of doing things for my children, and this was something that I missed. We feel limited by inmate restrictions.*

*It gave me an opportunity to hear the pain others experienced as an incarcerated parent, which validated my experience.*

*It has been a forum for coming together as men to discuss our issues.*

Parenting programs that provide parents with tools to improve the quality of parent-child relationships and learn non-coercive discipline have demonstrated to be effective in reducing behavior problems (Patterson, Mockford, & Stewart-Brown, 2005). Parents will positively influence their children's behavior by utilizing suitable discipline techniques that will encourage appropriate behaviors in various situations. Sample activities include: hugs, social praise, rewards, consequences, discussing problems, and establishing clear behavioral expectations, rules and routines. It is important to avoid the use of negative discipline techniques such as: yelling, threatening to punish, and spanking.

In addition, to practicing positive communication and discipline techniques parenting programs must also incorporate the importance of instilling respect. Respect is a value that parents strived to instill in their children (Yearwood & McClowry, 2008). Sample activities incarcerated parents can engage in to raise respectful children include modeling, and identifying and discussing traits and behaviors that will encourage children to treat people appropriately. It will need to include the importance of teaching children to respect elders family, and others in the community. The parents and the child will clearly define appropriate ways to interact with authority figures, supervisors, and school personnel.

## Conclusion

Thus far you can see the impact of incarceration on the family as well as how it directly impacts the life of a child at home and in school. The child of an incarcerated parent may feel the absence of any physical affection or emotional connection from their parent for years. The parenting role and responsibilities of incarcerated parents are significantly impacted by criminal justice policies and practices. Incarceration impacts the parent-child relationship; it could have devastating effects (behaviorally, socially, psychologically, and academically) for a lifetime for both the parent and the child. Parents in prison are raising their children through letters, telephone conversations and during prison visitation. The types of interactions parents in prison have with their child or their decision making abilities concerning the child is dependent upon the support of correctional facilities, the custodial parent, schools, and members of the community.

It is important for custodial parents to identify ways to motivate their child's school to take a leading role in educating the community about the impact of parental incarceration on children and families. It will be advantageous for families experiencing incarceration to have all stakeholders to become actively involved in identifying programs and services that may prevent these children from certain risks such as poverty, trouble with the law, and behavioral issues in school or in their community. To increase the success of children with an incarcerated parent, the collaboration of the stakeholders include courts, prisons, community organizations, social service agencies, schools, and policymakers are needed to effectively develop and implement programs that will address their needs and to provide appropriate and relative support services.

Furthermore, the parents' that participate in parenting programs significantly increases their opportunity to positively influence their child's life as well as the relationships within the family. The support and positive interaction amongst the family will reduce the chances of returning to prison intergenerational incarceration, and ultimately increase the child's chances for a better professional and personal life.

# Chapter 6:
# Parent Involvement with Their College Young Adult

## Dr. Lynn B. Elfe

### Introduction

As parents we do not need a lot of money and education to make our children scholars. Some very successful and important scholars have come from meager backgrounds and they have made their mark on the world.

Dr. Ben Carson lived in an inner city, in dire poverty, and in a single parent home. His mother had a third-grade education but she knew what to do to have her sons do better in school. She limited their TV watching. It worked because Dr. Carson graduated from Yale in 1973. He then enrolled in the School of Medicine at the University of Michigan, choosing to become a neurosurgeon. At the young age of 33 he became director of pediatric neurosurgery at Johns Hopkins Hospital. In 1987, Dr. Carson attracted international attention by performing a surgery to separate 7-month-old craniopagus twins from Germany.

Shaquille O'Neal was born in Newark, New Jersey. Estranged from his biological father, his mother Lucille O'Neal married Phillip Harrison when Shaquille was 3. During O'Neal's youth, the family moved to Army bases in New Jersey, Georgia West Germany, and then Fort Sam Houston in San Antonio Texas. He became a star NBA player, actor, and rapper. Note that even with his celebrity status he thought education was important to pursue. He graduated from Louisiana State University, Baton Rouge, LA with a BS in General Studies, in 2000. He received his MBA in 2005 from the University of Phoenix; and in 2012, he received his EdD, from Barry University, Miami Shores, FL.

John Quiñones, grew up in a Spanish-speaking household and did not learn English until he started school at age 6. Determined to overcome the current Hispanic stereotypes of being uneducated, he decided to attend college. After graduating from Brakenridge High School, Quiñones went to St. Mary's University where he joined an Upward Bound program, a Federal TRIO program preparing him for college. After graduating from St. Mary's with a bachelor's degree in Speech Communications, he earned his master's degree from Columbia University's School of Journalism. Presently, John Quiñones is the anchor of "What Would You Do?" It is one of the highest-rated newsmagazine franchises of recent years. During his 25-year tenure at ABC News, he has reported extensively for all programs and platforms and served as anchor of "Primetime."

Drs. Sampson Davis, Rameck Hunt, and George Jenkins have been called The Three Doctors. They are an extraordinary example of leadership and determination. They grew up on the challenging inner-city streets of Newark, New Jersey where the three teenagers made a pact. They decided to stick together, go to college, graduate, and become doctors. Because the negative influences were in their everyday lives and positive role models were fleeting, the teenagers' journey was challenging, but successful. The Three Doctors have overcome adversity and succeeded in writing books, being major motivational speakers, and serving as the face of health and education for youth and families across the country.

Dr. Maya Angelou experienced the brutality of racial discrimination. Born Marguerite Annie Johnson, Angelou survived a difficult childhood. Her parents split up when she was very young, and she and her older brother Bailey were sent to live with their father's mother, Anne Henderson, in Stamps, Arkansas. At age 14 Maya dropped out of school to become San Francisco's first Black female cable car conductor. Soon thereafter she became a single mother who supported her son by working as a waitress and a cook. Her passion for the arts took hold and Dr. Angelou became a celebrated poet, memoirist, novelist, educator, dramatist, producer, actress, historian, filmmaker, and civil rights activist.

It is possible to create a scholar even if you are the parent in one of the poorest households in town. With a plan, it is possible to find the formula that works for any child. That plan has to include determination from a caregiver. It also has to include a plan of: time, attention, intention and love. This plan has to be implemented all the way from pre-school through the college years. Yes parents, through your child's college years.

When our children are in the lower grades, their parental needs are not so different from their needs when they arrive at the high school steps and then at the college curb. If you think about it, most parents have been saying the same thing to their child from the first homework assignment in pre-school to the last paper they write before graduation. As a parent you have been telling your child to get up and go to school and then when they return you tell them to do their homework. You have been asking them about their school day and what they need for the next day. Once they finish their first thirteen years of school they still need our guidance: academically, socially, financially medically, and emotionally, for at least one or two more years of their college experience.

Essentially, when your son or daughter goes off to college, you are leaving your child with people they do not know and more importantly, these are people you do not know. You have no information about the college representatives your child has talked to so far. Your child has probably shared their vital information with admissions and guidance counselors as well as financial aid staff. You know nothing about these people.

Over the years, you have told your child not to talk to strangers. You have probably emphasized it whenever they left the house. Now that they are going off to college, the people you are entrusting your child to are complete strangers. They are strangers to you and strangers to your child. Your child is going to be working with new people who are going to be shaping their lives. In essence, you have no idea how these people will treat your child, what their values of life are, or their life's point of view. You don't know if they are positive and encouraging or if they will even like your child. These are critical reasons why a parent cannot just drop their child off at the college door and why parents need to keep continued communication with their young adult.

If your child is commuting to the campus, it is probably a place where they may have only seen once, when they had to attend the admissions interview or a quick tour. You don't know anything about the safety of the campus. For instance, what are the parking lots like? Are they lit well? Where does your child go if there is an emergency? Again, think about it, without having these answers, you are still allowing your child to attend the campus.

When you drop your child off on a college campus as a residential student, your child will be residing in a new living situation with other students they do not know. They won't know their roommates' eating habits, cleanliness routines, religious views, or common sense level. You do not know the resident assistants who are ultimately, just students themselves. You would hope that they will be fair and responsible, but again, they are just someone else's child who may be one or two years older than yours. You don't know your child's financial needs, and new ways of living. They are now paying for books. That is something that was not a part of the high school budget. They may be paying dues to be a member of a club, or paying someone to edit a paper. You want to make sure your child will thrive in this new place. So parents, your child still needs your love and attention.

## Academically

The parent has to pay attention. Pay attention to who this child is academically. Does your child write letters backward or upside-down? If they have some kind of disability, there is help to assist you and your child in their quest to be a scholar. What is your child's learning style? Do they learn better sitting in a room where there are other activities? Is your child more comfortable working alone behind a closed door? Is your child more productive working on two or more projects at one time? As long as you assist them in finding a place to study and the tools to study with, you are paying attention to the needs of your scholar-to-be.

Your high school student needs to know that their parents are still interested in their learning. In high school the parents still need to know does my child have the tools to do the best they can? Is my child getting the assistance they need to succeed? As your child enters college you still need to be able to answer those questions. You also need to know if your child is spending the necessary time in their books to maintain the grades they will need, so they can move closer to the future of their choice. After all, this is a huge investment for you as a parent. You need to know if they are doing the right thing to help secure your investment. When your young adult is in college, the focus of your concern may be a little different, but you still need to be able to answer those same questions that we asked ourselves as they moved through the high school process. Now that they are in college the students still need to know that their parents are still their strongest supporters. Even if the parents did not attend college and do not know the process themselves, the students need to know that they can communicate openly and that their parents are still willing to assist them. There are some parts of the process that are logical and common sense will guide you to make sure they are going to the right people in a timely manner as they make decisions about courses and majors.

Socially

Our children have a great deal of freedom once they are off to college. If your child is a college commuter student, you don't know what they are doing as they go in and out of the doors of your home. To keep them grounded you still need to know who they are hanging out with. If they live on the campus, parents do not know what their child is doing from one day to another, unless there is open communication. You still need to know what they are doing in their free time. You still want to impart your words of wisdom so they can hear your voice over their shoulder as they venture out of your comfort zone.

Financially

Parents need to be there as your young adults begin to manage their own finances. Before they can get to freshman year, they need you to assist them with that infamous FAFSA (Free Application for Federal Student Assistance). They will have to navigate the student loan system with your guidance and signature. If you don't know how to go about it, then you and your college student can learn the process together. Here are some other financial questions for you to consider as you send your child off to college. What immediate cash do you have in your wallet to assist your child? Will your child work on campus or off campus? Will your young adult have a credit card? If so, have you explained the benefits and dangers of utilizing credit cards? Will they have a car? If they do, will you share in the cost? What is your young adult's level of financial literacy? They will still need some parental involvement to make their journey to be a scholar as painless as possible. Communication is key.

Medically

When our young adults enter college they must have a completed, satisfactory medical report in their hand. Even with that clean bill of health, we still need to check on their health during the semesters. If they are living on a campus, there are all kinds of possible illnesses the students pass along to each other. With long study hours and many working hours, often the lack of sleep can take a toll on students' bodies. Mononucleosis is a college ailment that is very common and it can knock your child off their feet. One week of missing college classes can put your student in jeopardy of losing a semester of grades and financial aid. Many college students have a new found freedom and it would be important to make sure our children are often informed of alcohol related medical concerns and sexually transmitted diseases. Again, open communication with our young adult college student is imperative.

Emotionally

As a high school student, your child needs to talk with you about their goals for their future. What do they like to do? What are they good at and can they make a living doing either of these? They need assistance thinking about a college major and parents are the people who usually know their college bound students best. Parents may not know the details of the majors, but they will be able to get some idea by doing some light research. The student needs assistance thinking about what college to attend in what part of the world, financial aid, the impact on the family members, and other possibilities if college is not a part of their plan. They need our continued assistance in so many aspects of their young lives, as they leave high school, and embark on the next phase of their young lives.

In the period between the high school graduation and the beginning of the freshman semester, the only thing that has changed is time. This child is still our "baby", nervous about making a mistake; nervous about making decisions that will affect their lives; nervous about all the new situations they will encounter. Do not think you can just drop them off on campus and let them fend for themselves as young adults. That high school student is still looking for the parental support as a college student and you have not completed your quest to create a scholar.

Your children encounter situations in college that they could have never expected. Have we prepared them for disappointments with relationships, foiled friendships unexpected poor grades or racial incidents with administrators and students? Poor decisions are just some of the situations that can take a toll on the hearts of our children. All of these situations are in need of a parent's touch to keep them strong and confident so they can have the persistence to continue.

## Provide Positive Role Models

As a parent, we are our child's first role model. They see the things we do. They see if we are consistent and if we keep our word. They see if we are fair and if we are vengeful. They listen to the things we say to others. When we are angry with them, they notice how we treat them. They were watching to see if you were going to return the change when the cashier gave you too much. What have you modeled for your child? Here are questions parents can ask themselves as they wonder if they have modeled behavior that will allow their child to be able to cope in the next phase of their life. These are also questions parents can ask themselves as they assess how well they have prepared their high school student to be a college freshman.

*Academically,* did you create a study routine for your child? Did you make it known that school was first, then play? Were you consistent when you set a rule?

*Socially,* have you showed your child the appropriate behaviors when in a crowd of people? Does your child know the social graces because they have seen you demonstrate them?

*Financially,* have you shown good money management? Have you demonstrated responsible paying of bills and the proper use of credit cards?

*Medically* have you visited your doctors on a regular basis and have you modeled a body of good health? Do you smoke and then expect them not to? Are you a drinker? Do you drink in moderation and your child sees you drinking responsibly? Have you taught your child about their body and how to recognize when their body is not well? Did you teach your child the importance of good nutrition and moderation and demonstrate that behavior?

*Emotionally,* have you given your child the tools to be able to stand up for his or herself? Have you showed them what it looks like to be politically correct and yet still show your personal strength? Does your child have the self-esteem and confidence to withstand a personal attack? Have you modeled behavior that has allowed your child to know just how important they are to you and to the world?

You can always find other field experts, life coaches, and distinguished people to be role models for your child, but you are the one who sets the standard in the most important aspects of the child's life. Their self-respect, dignity, and integrity are developed with your nurturing. Then your child will model what they see you do. You have the ability to create the scholar by affording your child time and attention with intention and love.

It is important for your child to have role models. The role model can be the person who owns the shop on the corner. The person in the neighborhood who owns his own construction company can be the role model. The person who lives next door who is the CPA and works from home is a model for entrepreneurship. The same people going out every morning to go to different jobs can be your child's role models. Your child needs to see an abundance of the possibilities for their future.

Who are the college students in your neighborhood? They are home for breaks and mini vacations. Set up a moment when they can spend some time with your child to talk about the college experience. They could be role models as your child decides whether college is the experience they want to strive for. They may decide that particular experience is not for them. College can take on many forms. Would they prefer a 2-year instead of a 4-year institution? Would they prefer to be a commuter student by night, so they can pursue a work experience that suits their desire by day? Or maybe your child has decided college is not for them. Perhaps they want to pursue a different path of certificates from career institutes. These students can be considered scholars too. Their journey will just look a little different. Remember the adage "it takes a village"? All of the people in your neighborhood can assist as your child tries to figure out what they will do with their future.

## Communication and Life Mentoring

Mentoring has been described as a relationship between two people. Even in some elementary schools mentoring programs exist to provide youngsters with role models who help a child develop socially and emotionally. Mentors help children learn to understand and communicate their feelings, to relate to their peers, and to develop relationships with other adults. Mentoring involves "personal and professional networking counseling, guiding, instructing, modeling and sponsoring. It was a developmental mechanism," (Tillman, 2001, p. 296). It has been described as a support system of communication and socialization (Holmes, Land, & Hinton-Hudson, 2007; Tillman 2001).

The traditional form of mentoring consists of one person who has a great deal of knowledge and experience in an area and is willing to impart that information upon a less experienced individual, the protégé, in a hierarchical relationship. Mentors wear many hats. They act as delegators, role models cheerleaders, policy enforcers, advocates, and friends.

For older students, the research shows that mentoring enhances the academic learning by affording the students the opportunity to associate with industry professionals and people with diverse thinking. The mentor relationship can assist the student in acquiring career guidance and making valuable connections that could last a lifetime. There are many benefits of mentoring for students by connecting students to the professional community, by providing career networking opportunities, and by helping students with career planning.

As a parent, you can provide the forum for your child to have this opportunity. There may be programs in your community or around your community that will not charge the parent for these services. You will need to do the research to see what is available and appropriate for your child. One place where you can begin to research is the Young Men's or Young Women's Christian Association (YMCA/YWCA). If you are a member, you may already have access to these services. Many towns have an Education Opportunity Center (EOC) and the Education Assistance Corp (EAC) program. Additionally, other community organizations or local churches may sponsor a Big Brothers Big Sisters, Catholic Charities, or your community church. Often, the high school will be able to assist you. Some high schools have programs like SMART Scholars; Upward Bound; Gear Up; Science, Technology, Engineering and Math (STEM); and Science and Technology Entry Program (STEP). The nearby colleges may have a program where your children may have access to a mentor.

As our student decides to move forward with their academic endeavors they will still need parents to continually reinforce a belief in their abilities, their self-concept, and bolster their self-esteem. We must not assume that our child does not need our supportive words. Their abilities will be challenged as they learn to study differently, adjust to a different type of schedule and a different environment. As they realize they are going to have to make day-to-day decisions without the parent's voice in the background, they will need to know that they can confer with an encouraging adult, preferably the parent.

## Student Transition to College

Often a high school graduate is only 17 years old and the only educational experience they have had is their high school. The only life experience they have had is with their immediate family and their community. For the most part, the only difference between a student who graduates from high school and a student who becomes a freshman in college is about two months. They graduate from high school in June and they begin college in August. In that small amount of time, most students are working for the summer to earn money. They are not preparing themselves for the transition to their new academic setting.

If this student is the first in their family to attend college then the student doesn't have a solid base from which to fall back on. The student may not have had the opportunity to have a conversation with a family member to discuss what to expect from the experience. In a study conducted by Rhoda Miller and Stephanie Tatum (2006) it was found that "cultural change is a problem encountered by first-generation students regarding the discomforts that arise upon leaving the social standing of one's family of orientation" (p. 41). So it is important for these students to remain connected to home for the cultural and emotional support of family.

Hopefully, these young adults do attend an orientation program of some kind, so they can begin to see the different picture of the different kind of family they will become a part of in that different college community. Research shows that summer programs do assist these students with a smoother transition to their new environment. The transition to college can have its challenges. "There is a significant amount of adjustment that must take place in the transition to any undergraduate institution" (Hurtado, Carter, & Spuler, 1996, p. 136).

This is the time when the parents need to make sure they keep in touch with their young adults. Parents may not have thought about whether they have supplied their children with the tools they need to succeed in this new environment. In fact, do the parents know what tools they supplied their children with for elementary, middle school, and high school? Do the parents know what the educational experience was like for their child in high school? Is this something parents talked about with their child? As a parent, did you know if the child felt challenged academically? Were they struggling in high school? Did the child go to a diverse high school and experience different cultures? As a parent, did you think it was important for the child to live in a homogeneous neighborhood, a neighborhood where everyone looked just like them? As a parent, what did you tell your child about people who were different? The research shows that it is important for students to think about the environment from which they came as they venture away from a familiar type of community to something out of their knowledge base. Is this something you as a parent discussed with your child and how will this information affect their transition to college?

In this day and age parents must give their child the information about the reality of a global society. After all, "The world is flat!", says Thomas L. Friedman (2007), the author of *The World is Flat 3.0*. In his book, Freidman (2007) explains:

> . . . what the flattening of the world means is that we are now connecting all the knowledge centers on the planet together into a single global network, which—if politics and terrorism do not get in the way—could usher in an amazing era of prosperity, innovation, and collaboration by companies, communities, and individuals. (p. 8)

As parents, we want our children to be a part of this flattening. These children have access to other nations with the Internet. Students are playing games with students from other countries. High schools are sending their students abroad to immerse themselves in the culture as they learn different languages. They are participating in more internships abroad, making friends with students from foreign countries, and bringing these new friends home. It becomes important for your child to have information about these other cultures. This is just one of the concepts of the transition to college that needs to be thought about for a college bound student.

**Student Quotes**

I have obtained first-hand information from research I have conducted with college students. These college students shared their experiences as they transitioned to college. Some of the students also shared the kind of communications they had with their parents and the supportive needs they felt were necessary for their successful change to the college environment. Most of these students who were interviewed lived far enough away that they needed to reside on the campus. The commuter students also shared their experiences as they made their transition to college.

The students I spoke with were Black young men and women who were on a predominately White college campus. Even though their responses may be specific to their situation, I feel it is important for all parents to know that their child could be faced with challenging situations that could frustrate them intimidate them, or leave them very confused and/or depressed if they did not have parental support. Have you prepared your child for these types of circumstances? Does your child feel you are available to support them in their time of need, even though they may now be considered a young adult?

The students I interviewed were from different backgrounds. Some of these Black students were from high schools and communities that were diverse. Many of these students felt more than prepared to venture out into the world of differences. They grew up in predominately Black communities and schools where they thrived. Some experienced good relationships in predominately White communities and schools while others did not advance as well in the predominately White institution and community. The students talked with me about their experiences in this new college environment with no hesitation. They shared their feelings of comfort or discomfort while being on a predominately White college campus. The quotes on the following pages also express their connections with their parents.

I spoke with students about their transition to college and found some interesting information. Here is a quote from a young college student who came from a very diverse community. This student lived on campus and articulated that even though they felt pretty well prepared for the transition to college, the need for the support from home was still evident.

Freshman year I went home a lot, just because my Mom and I were really close. But then in my sophomore year I got more involved and started getting even more involved with the organizations and bonding with my fellow classmates. Overall it was just a different experience. We were a graduating class of 60 students in high school. Here it will be 6,000 students. I enjoyed the numbers of people.

An important part of this quote is the relationship with the parent. The transition to college included many trips home, not because anything bad had happened on the campus, and not because the student was having any identifiable adjustment issues. For this freshman sleeping in their own bed on the weekends was important. Maybe the student just needed the emotional support from familiar surroundings or the knowledge that there was still a place they could go to regain their sense of balance. This student needed that freshman year to find their footing at the college so they could then feel comfortable to get involved in the campus activities. This parent made it conducive for the student to come home until such time as the student became comfortable enough to make the campus their new temporary home.

Because the student is going into a new environment they cannot predict what situations may arise. This next student had grown up in a predominately Black community where the schools were also predominately Black. In high school, this student was well revered socially, academically, and athletically. Now entering the grounds of a predominately White institution the student could not be prepared for the different type of treatment that he or she would experience. This student's quote expresses the need to be connected with the family because the student experienced some racial situations that made it difficult to acclimate him or her to the new environment.

Initially when I came here, I'm not even gonna lie to you, I felt, I think culture shock from the very beginning. To be honest with you, I was always

on the phone with my parents every day, just
because I felt very uncomfortable, like, [from] the
coach on down.

This student had the need for family support. Whether it
was a physical connection or a familiar voice on the phone, we
cannot presume that our children will be settled in a new
environment without the family support. Whether the student
was asking the parents for strategic guidance or a shoulder to cry
on, the phone calls were necessary for the student to remain
grounded to persist in this college environment.

This next quote was taken from a student who had a
belief of the world due to the wonderfully safe diverse high
school experience. Once in college the realization that the home
community experience was not going to be duplicated at the
college became clear, and that this home away from home was
going to be inundated with racial tension. This understanding
rocked the student.

I think I was kind of like spoiled and my growing
up in my high school was awesome because the
town I came from was very, very diverse. You
have people at lower socioeconomic status and
then like higher economic status all living
together and the Black, White, Spanish, like
everything all mixed up together and everybody
got along like there was very few like, racial
tensions at all. And I guess, growing up, that you
believe that's kind of how the world is.

So the questions parents have to ask themselves is: Did I prepare
my child for this type of circumstance? Does my child have the
skills to recover from the disillusion of a life of fairness and to
manage diversity of an environment with racial tension? Parents
cannot know how their child will respond to the new
environment. Parents cannot know how the new environment
will treat or mistreat their child who was dropped off at the front
door of the new college home. Parents cannot know if their child

will be able to concentrate on the academic rigors at hand and still have this troubling situation on their mind. Being there as a buffer, an ear, a problem solver could be the reassurance the student needs to move through another day. This is one of the reasons why it is important to keep in contact with the college student.

This next quote came from a student who embraced the differences of the campus and found a new understanding about a group of people that otherwise would not have been explored.

> It was really different. I mean, I came from a place where everybody was Black and now I am here on a White university. I thought everybody here was Jewish when I first came here. Like they celebrated the Jewish holidays and I became interested in what the Jewish people did. I became friends with a Jewish kid so I went with them to their different things to see what it was. I enjoyed it.

Even though this student found comfort in this newfound culture we cannot be sure whether the parents had any knowledge of this interest. Would they approve? Would they be concerned? Would they share the student's excitement? Depending on the relationship these parents had with their child when the student became a member of this college community will determine whether the student even mentioned this interest to the parents. If the parents were supportive of this student's interest or not, it is always advantageous to know what the student is doing with their free time.

As a parent of a student who is living away from home there may not be a great deal of control you can have about what your child will be doing from one moment to another. They have now become the young adult who is a little bit different from the young adult you knew just a few months ago. However, if there is some level of support, understanding, and communication from the parents, at least, you will have an inkling of what the student will decide to be involved with and how the student will spend their time. The parent may still want to impart some words of wisdom, some heartfelt concern as the student moves forward with the campus involvement and personal independence. Sometimes the student may get advice from their parents that are meant to be helpful but the student may interpret this information in a manner that actually holds the student back from getting fully involved with the campus and the possibilities of growth. Parents want to make sure that the students think of all aspects of an environment and they want their young student to be cautious and safe. The parent talks from their life's experience and hope that their child will take heed to the information that they impart to their child. Having a relationship with open communication is not always easy, but then again, this whole transition may not be easy. It is just inevitable.

It is important for the parent to pass along this information and it is important that the parent continue to make sure that their student has considered the information that the parent has given. Because the young adult has his or her own way of thinking, it is important that the parent engage in conversation to assist their child in processing the information. The student explained

> It was really different. I had never been in a school that was all White before. I remember it was funny when I told my father. He is a little bit of a racist. He told me well you better watch yourself because they are going to want to keep you down. Somehow I got by. I mean I didn't have that many friends freshman year, but it was alright.

Did this student just "get by" because they were thinking about the comment their father made? Did the student take the comment to heart and keep isolated? Did the student look for people who were trying to keep them down and avoid them? It is hard to know how the student took this information if the parent did not continue to have open communication.

## Parents Want Their Children to Fit In

When our children first go off to pre-school and kindergarten, we hope they will get along with the other children. After all, they will be spending most of their daytime hours engrossed in the group dynamics of that academic community. Often, how our children fare with other children is a direct reflection on the skills we have given them to fit in with their peers. As they move from elementary school to middle school we expect that there will come a time when they may have a squabble or two with other children every once in a while. We also feel responsible for making sure our children have the ability to solve those quarrels and maintain those relationships. By the time they have entered high school, we expect and hope our children have found their place in the crowd, made friends and can enjoy their days in their school community.

All of these years we have been by our children's side giving them the words they need to hear to feel strong enough to fight their battles, to maneuver the study situations and all of their after school activities. Then they become old enough to choose a new environment where they will study and in many cases live, without the immediate presence and supervision of their parents. We can only hope that we have given them all of the tools they need to fit in.

There is much research about college students fitting in. One such researcher, is Banning (1978). He identified the importance of studying "the relationship between the student and the campus environment" (p. 5). Another researcher, Tinto (1993) referred to this phenomenon as the Person-Environment Fit (P-E Fit). P-E Fit was a way to quantify how a person felt about his or her acceptance within a specific setting. It also spoke to the connection that the individual had to that specific setting (Swartz-Kulstad & Martin, 2000). P-E Fit had the potential to affect a student's adjustment to campus life. In Tinto's model of student departure, he stated that the P-E Fit level, both academically and socially, impacted a student's decision to stay or leave a college. His model of student departure explained that higher P-E Fit levels in these two areas lead to greater student satisfaction. Greater student satisfaction increased the probability that the student would remain in college (Tinto, 1993). I would like to add that from the information I have gathered from students, part of this fit and students' decision to stay or go has a lot to do with the relationship with the parents during their college days. The following student says that they felt the difference all around them.

> It was a different mentality. So it was like their ideas were so foreign. The way they talked was different. The things they liked were different. So that's when I became more like introverted, cause it was like, I don't really fit in.

This student quoted below found an outlet on the campus that assisted with the student's sense of connectedness, and therefore became an active part of the college community.

> At first it was just like, going back into being at high school. Where it is like, I don't know where I fit in, but through [Multicultural Program], I started meeting people. I'm involved with [Multicultural Program]. I am an active member.

Similar to the situation with the above student, many college students, especially freshmen, are looking for a place to call home on the campus. In the student's statement below, the student even calls the head of the Multicultural Program "Mama" before her actual name.

> I say give pounds to Mama [name]. She always tells us to do the right thing. Do this, do that. She makes us take the initiative to settle things. I just feel like we are the ones who have to make it better. We are the ones who have to put reason to things while they just disrespect us. I do this [attend activities sponsored by the multicultural program], probably because I've been deprived of people of color. Yes, I've never gotten to

participate in anything during middle school or
high school. I've made a step team once, showing
kids how to step, but it's not the same as being
part of people who already know, who can teach
me something    as well as the teaching me
something new.

And still another student mentions that they were looking for a
place that they could call home on the campus.

It has been a major role. I think in part from me
just being me and I tried to adapt to any
environment. I don't think my experience would
have been as pleasant if we didn't have this office
to turn to. I don't think I experienced any
professor treating me differently because I'm
Black, but I would say that I would not have
loved it here if any of the organizations' of
multicultural were not here. If we didn't have
somewhere to turn to that we could call home, I
don't know what we would have done. We were
here 24/7, but if we didn't have this, we probably
would not be unified, but we probably wouldn't
feel like we mattered either.

Another student explained how important it is to find a place on
the campus that makes them feel comfortable, a place where they
can be themselves and know that they will receive good
information from a person who cares about them. This student
has found a place on the college campus that has the
characteristics of home. This student stated:

We are always here because this is the meeting
place. And even before the office is opened in the
morning, this is the place that works for us. We
come to this office if I need help on anything. I
can talk to [name]. She will put me in the right
direction and tell me what to do and how to do it.

So the next time I can handle it on my own. I
know even if it's not me or if someone else that I
know who's in trouble, if you need something I
know that I can also point them to her. Like all
these books around here. They are for the book
club but any student can come in here and borrow
any of these books. If someone cannot afford a
book, then they can come here and borrow it. A
ride home, come here to figure it out. This is the
place to come.

So even though these students were old enough to leave home
and did not have their parents at a close proximity, they were still
in need of those distinctive characteristics of a home away from
home. Parents may not be contacted by their students each and
every day, but they will need to know that the parent will be
there when their child needs them.

When I interviewed many of the students, I could sense
that they were responsible students who were independent and
getting things done. They were working, socializing, being
involved in campus activities, managing their time. and obtaining
good grades. Yet they still felt it was important to have a
place/person they could go to who would treat them with the
tender loving care they were use to from their parents. Another
student explained:

Whatever I wanted to do, he [the advisor] was
definitely behind me 110%, but there wasn't the
connection where he would go above and beyond.
He probably would have done the work anyway.
But after talking to an adviser as opposed to
talking to [Director of Multicultural Program ] she
tried to get down beyond the surface and find out
exactly what it is that I want and help me to write
my essay for scholarships or edit something for
me as opposed to him just saying that's good,
send it off. It wasn't that they were not supportive
but they didn't go above and beyond. She,
[Director of Multicultural Program ], was

passionate. She is passionate about every student, so you never feel like she's gonna get more attention than me . . . you know. So I think that would be the difference.

The research states, "Creating a campus climate in which students feel they belong and are valued, challenged, and affirmed by their peers and teachers" (Kuh, 2001/2002. p. 23) appeared to be a promising strategy for improving persistence and graduation rates. Persistence in this case helps to describe a student's continuation behavior and process they attain that leads them to a desired goal of academic achievement. The students are looking for that support of the family, people who will make them feel safe and encouraging in times of need and they do this by making a home away from home.

## Parent Transition to College

Student success depends on a variety of factors. Parental involvement is one of those factors. In the prior reading you were informed that the student still needs your time, attention intention, and love. You are asked to have a working knowledge of what your child is going to be involved with on the campus and continue to be supportive in their quest to complete college. If your child is going to be living on a campus, you are asked to be connected and expect that they will need your continued support, sometimes more than others. If your student is a commuter student, it is important that you allow them the necessary time and freedom to persist.

First-generation college students often find that because their parents do not know what the process entails, the parent is uncomfortable with some of the students' requests. The parents are used to the child being home in the evenings because that is what they did when they were in high school. They had chores to complete and family obligations to uphold. The parents see their high school student and many times they do not recognize the student's need for a slight change of plans.

As a director of a college program, I am learning from

experience that often the parent of a first-generation college student, who is a commuter, goes through their own transition that leads to some family complexities. I have witnessed, what I have labeled, the "Feeling Inadequate Parent." Because this parent has not had this college experience, often they cannot answer a lot of the student's questions and are uncomfortable that their child is moving into a life that they do not know much about. I have experienced the "Feeling Jealous Parent." This parent realizes that their child is now embarking on a future that they were never privy to and they may have some feelings of resentment.

From time to time I have witnessed the "Crying Parent." This parent has mixed emotions about their child moving into the next phase of their life. They are dealing with "my baby is growing up." There is the "Out of Control Parent." This parent has decided that, they are going to keep their child from transitioning into this new life. They want their child to remain the person that they have been and no matter how unreasonable their request, they find every way possible to make the student's life difficult. No, you cannot study with your classmate, come home. No, you cannot go to that student event in the evening even though there are administrators and professors there. No you cannot go to the school to bond and learn more about what other students are doing to succeed, on a day when you do not have class.

There is the "Selfish Parent." This parent wants the student to major in a field that they believe is most lucrative even if the student's interests are in some other area. Granted we do not want our student to have a degree in an area that may be risky, but we cannot expect them to be just like us. This is a good time to talk with the students about possibilities, not demand that they create a future that may not be to their liking.

There is also the "Protective Parent." This is the parent with the helicopter cap on their head. You know the parent who continues to be hovering around the every move that the student makes. This parent may drop the student off at the school before class and pick them up after they are finished with work. This parent wants to try to keep tabs on their child just as they did in high school to make sure the student is doing everything they are suppose to be doing and checking that the homework assignments are in their book bag and their lunch is in the bag too. Although we as administrators are excited that the parent is concerned for their child, we are hoping that this student can find their way around the campus on their own. This parent has to realize that the transition is on and the student and the parent have to navigate this change together.

Many of these parents are having difficulty with this new situation. The student has a new schedule, a new set of friends and a new focus. Your student may give you their schedule of classes and even though they have gaps in their day, they may have other projects or activities that they want to attend. Give them the permission to grow. They still need your support. They will not "out grow" the parent and the family life. They will just enhance it with their new experiences and possibilities for an adventurous future.

**Student Involvement**

The research shows that "student involvement refers to the amount of physical and psychological energy that the student devotes to the academic experience," (Astin, 1984, p. 518). Involved students were those who expended a significant amount of time studying, creating and maintaining relationships with their professors and their peers and participated in activities and programs on the campus. Astin also explained that involvement could take place along a scale with different students devoting different amounts of time to the campus. He explained, "being academically involved is strongly related to satisfaction with all aspects of college life, except friendships with other students" (p. 525).

Students want to please their parents. They want their parents to know that they are using their hard earned money to the fullest. The student quoted below is integrating into his or her campus.

I started meeting people. There was this one student. He was always pushing me like you should come to [organization]. You are going to be glad to meet other people. I was kind of hesitant. I was really nervous. Now I am involved in [organization] but more importantly I am the secretary. I really like doing this.

Astin (1984) further stated that, "simply by eating, sleeping, and spending their waking hours on the college campus, residential students have a better chance than do commuter students of developing a strong identification and attachment to undergraduate life" (p. 523). He also explained that those students, who became members of fraternities or sororities and involved themselves in extracurricular activities, including sports, were more likely to persist and stay in college.

As a parent, we want our child to fit in to their new environment. College is a time for the students to explore and figure out what new things interest them and where they will fit in best. A student stated,

Campus Activity Board does really great things. Like recently we just had a bowling competition which I heard was absolutely great. I didn't partake in it just because it was during a time that was not OK for me. But then they had another event that you have to make stuffed animals and I thought that was absolutely amazing. So I mean it just depends on what the event is. I am an all-purpose event participant . . . OOOO Did I say that?

The student quoted above has found that there are different things that are of interest. Being a part of new adventures can still be scary. As parents, we want to be able to encourage our children to look into many different endeavors. College is a time of exploration and decision making for a future that will be best for them. This student stated,

I do actually. Well I try to. I attend a lot of the concerts and then the events through

Multicultural. Recently they had the trip to Montreal. We went to the diversity conference. That was fun. One of my friends is a poet. She invited me to one of the events she had. So I try to get to that kind of stuff too. I also participate in the AIA American Institute for the Arts. I enjoy the arts a lot.

On a college campus you will have all kinds of students attend classes. There are many kinds of non-traditional students. You will see the older student. The mother who has been home with the children all of these years and is now ready to create her own career. The businessman who has to make a change in his career and needs a certificate or degree to move forward is now on the campus. The military person who has returned home and is looking to start a new life is on the campus. There are also those young males and females who have babies and know how important it is to create a future for themselves and their young child. Because they are young parents they want to feel that they can fit into this college environment also. Sometimes the college falls short of making these non-traditional students feel welcomed. This non-traditional student states:

> There is no reason for me to come and join anything. They should have something for me too. Something for me to be able to bring my kid here to see, hey your [parent is going to school]. I am proud to be here. I don't feel that they are proud to have me here.

My experience has shown me that there are responsible young men who have a child and are trying to make their way as a student and a working dad. And of course there are those young mothers who are trying to be successful in academia while raising their child. In cases like these, we are hoping that these young people have families who are supporting these non-traditional student's academic endeavors and emotional needs.

## Relationships With Other Students

We are living in a very changing diverse world. On any campus there will be international students from all parts of the globe. Professors are visiting from different countries and our students are studying abroad. Understanding that diversity lives there are still those who fall back on old habits and old, faulty thinking, even mothers. Another student said,

> Most of my friends, now that I am talking about it, are like us. Actually friends . . . they are us. Some people don't click because they are too different and I guess everyone has their different views on things and the other person doesn't agree. And so when things clash and ideas clash it does get ugly. One of the girls explained that she believed her stereotypes because her mother believes them. Well when we talked to her about how that didn't make sense, that she has to be her own person, she agreed. So she has changed her idea about who we Blacks are, but she won't tell her mother about that, I guess that is better than nothing. We are not living with her mother.

## Racial Incidents

When we leave our children at the college door, we do not know what will happen. We can only hope that these administrators, professors, staff members, and other students will treat our child the way we want them to be treated. Sometimes this does not happen. Even though we are a diverse country there are still too many people who are not mature or smart enough not to judge a person by the way they look. Unfortunately, this is not a perfect world and the colleges often are not a perfect place, and incidents will arise. This commuter student expressed dismay when they encountered an incident on the way to class. The student stated:

> You still have situations on campus where you
> walk past a group of White kids and you can tell
> the kids are stuck up and they won't even move
> out of your way. Like when you walk down the
> hall trying to get to class and they all, they're not
> gonna move.

Even though this incident does not seem overly offensive,
it is still a reminder that the student is in an environment that
may not be safe. Who do they go to so they can express their
concern? What can they request from a campus official to
address this incident? Having a parent's ear may lighten the load
for this student. Some parental advice on how to handle a
situation like this may be helpful at this point. Have you, as a
parent, given your child the necessary skills to handle a situation
of this nature?

In another racial incident, the student did not receive the
support from the campus authorities and had to phone home for
assistance. The student explained:

> I am in a suite with these girls, White, spoiled,
> young, rich girls. They didn't bother me much. I
> tried to get along. And yeah, you are right, I have
> not been around much, but I did take a break
> around midterm time last semester so I was in the
> dorm more. I decided that I was going to bring
> some friends over. We were going to cook dinner
> and then go out dancing. I could see they
> [roommates] were not happy. While cooking, I
> realized that the sink was stopped up. I noticed
> some dishes already in the sink and a little bit of
> water puddle around the drain. So I called
> maintenance.
>
> We finished with dinner and I cleaned up
> the best I could washing some stuff in the
> bathroom sink. Maintenance never got there so I
> left the girls a note not that they didn't know
> about it. I didn't come in that night. I stayed with

one of the other girls in town since we were out late. I went to my room to get a change of clothes to get ready to go back out to work, when I noticed that my UGGS [popular brand of footwear] had something in them. It was chicken grease. Someone had poured chicken grease in my boots. So of course no one knew what happened.

I called the RA's. They said they could not do anything since they did not know who did it and there was no proof. I told her one of them should take responsibility for my destroyed boots. I was so mad that I called my parents. They told me to call security. Well they said the same thing. I was almost ready to give in. I got kinda intimidated when they said they [roommates] didn't do it and there were no witnesses.

Now I am super mad. This is vandalism and racism not to be ignored. So I called my dad. He called the campus police. I don't know what he said, although I can imagine. They called the girls in and before you know it, one of the girls gave up the one who did it. She ended up getting thrown out of the dorms.

Fortunately for this student, there was support from home. Understanding that college is a time for students to learn how to handle difficult situations, there are times that life brings them intimidating circumstances that they may not be ready to encounter. We do not want our student to have such a traumatic experience that they have an arduous time trying to recover. We as parents still need to be on the alert for troubling situations.

Another student was taken aback by what was seen on the campus. The student explained:

We had an incident over the summer where there was a noose in a tree. It was like early in the morning before anybody could see it on the campus by the classes. A professor took it down because they didn't see the big deal about it. So

nobody was told about the incident because they
thought it was going to bring too much hate out.
So it just got left alone.

What should a student do in a situation like this? Their
gut feeling says that it is serious, but there is no one available at
the moment to confer with. The professor did nothing and the
student doesn't know whether to trust the professor's judgment.
Having a parental ear to communicate with in a time of possible
danger is important.

## Relationships with Professors

The larger the campus the harder it is to get to know the
professors and have the professors get to know your child.
Hopefully, you as a parent have been able to give your child the
skills to make themselves known in a crowd. This student says:

> I don't think I have any relationships with the
> professors. There are about fifty in the class and
> so we have this large amphitheatre. Like my
> teacher doesn't know me from anyone. They'll
> know my name, but it's not like we have a
> connection, but I know they'll recognize me. If I
> need something or ask them something, they will
> help.

With the variety of majors on a campus there are going to be a
variety of professors from different cultures. Along with this
diversity come many different teaching styles. Not all of these
teaching styles will meet the learning style of your child. We do
hope that the student has learned what their learning style is and
how to obtain the most in a classroom as they can with the
strategies they have learned along the way. In this next quote a
student explained:

> I have another professor for [course] and he is an
> OK guy. I don't think I would take him again if I

have the choice. Mainly because he talks really slowly when he does his lecture and I have to work really hard to pay attention to him. I followed a suggestion from my mom. Now I take excessive notes with colored pencils and creative outlines of information to keep my mind occupied.

This parent never went to college, but because of life experiences and parental logic, there is wisdom and common sense that has been imparted to this student.

From elementary, middle, and all the way through high school parents get to meet the teachers and have conferences. It was always important to make sure you as a parent communicated with your child's teacher and of course the teacher's responsibility was to inform the parent of the student's progress. Now that the student is in college, that communication no longer happens. In fact, the students sometimes find it difficult to have communication with their professors.

Even though they are in the classroom with the professor at least 3 hours a week, there are many other students who want to speak with the professor before and/or after class. It gets difficult to talk with the professor. The student will have to make an appointment to speak with the professor. Here's hoping that they can find an allotted available time, since most students do work. Many of the professors are not full time. The professor may be an adjunct who has a job in their field of study and no office on the campus. Trying to meet with these professors can be more than a challenge.

As a parent, have you stressed perseverance to your child? Have you explained how important it is to make sure they stand up for themselves and make themselves known to the important people on the campus? Have you explained that it doesn't matter if you like the professor or not, there is still a syllabus of requirements that have to be met? When a student does make a connection with a professor that relationship can only make the student's college experience that much richer. This student stated:

I really like my professor. He's by far one of the best professors I have because he's always entertaining. He wants us to get involved. He makes a playful atmosphere where you wanna come to class and where the learning is interesting.

## Relationships with Black Professors

Sometimes making that connection does have to do with the culture or race of the individuals. On a predominantly White campus, there are not that many Black professors. This Black student had a Black professor and they were able to make a connection.

It's a little different. I think it's because the way we communicate. It is like a sister-brother kind of thing. It wasn't like being in class or nothing like that. It's just a different vibe. I feel comfortable talking to her. So it is definitely a different kind of relationship. You know. You appreciate the time that they take to be upfront and honest with you. Like they let their guard down from being an authority and just want to help you with what's right.

## Relationships with Staff

I remember taking my daughter to college for her freshman year. Once we met her roommate and her roommate's family, I went looking for the other important people on the campus. I first found the woman who was responsible for cleaning the bathrooms and the residence halls. I introduced her to my child and found out a little about who she was and who she was to her family. I then introduced my daughter to the Resident Assistant (RA). This is the person who is responsible for the behavior of the students in her hall. Of course this person is only about a year or two older than my child, but I wanted to make sure she had a good feel for who I was and how I would expect my child to be treated. I continued with the cashiers and servers in the dining halls, the nurse, and the security guards who were standing in the area of the residence halls.

Even though I tried to make all of those positive connections, there was no guarantee that all would be well. However, I figured these people would remember my child's first encounter with them and the mother who showed concern was pleasant and complimentary. Most parents do not make that initial introduction. Trying to make a way for your child to have a good experience does not always turn out the way you wish. Here is a quote from a student who did not have a good experience once a situation did arise. The student explained:

> I did have a very bad experience which was probably one of the only negative experiences that I've had here. My roommate in my sophomore year was White and the rest of us were Black, so I don't know if that had anything to do with it. But she was a case and she did things very strangely. Like she would wake up early in the morning and turn on the radio and she was very distracting and one day we came home and found feces on the floor. So dealing with the residential life, they were not very helpful or supportive of us and what we were going through. So our parents had to get involved and she was removed from the room.

## Resilience

An important characteristic of any child is resilience. Merriam-Webster defines resilience as an ability to recover from or adjust easily to misfortune or change. If we apply that definition to our children, it is the inner strength that the child has that allows them to approach, engage, and proficiently meet the challenges and demands that are placed before them. Resilience is built on hope and self worth. These traits are planted in the children by the adults who believe in the importance of who their child is.

As a parent sends their child off to college it is important to ask themselves if resilience is something they have instilled in their child. Does your child have the confidence that it will take? Does your child have the fortitude, determination, the endurance and the self-confidence to persist? I interviewed a student who found that inner strength. This student stated:

> My parents were always fighting and my parents divorced and lived about twenty miles apart. I decided that I was going to be my best outside of the house. So I got good grades and wanted to have a lot of good references so I could go to whatever college I wanted to go to and major in whatever I wanted.

In spite of her or his parents' difficult relationship, this student found the strength to turn a possible traumatic event in her or his life towards a positive outcome. When a child has this strength imbedded in their soul, they can accomplish almost anything.

There may come a time in any college student's career when the path looks bleak. Being able to see another way to get back on the path shows determination, something that this student had in her or his heart. The ability to think outside the box and make the impossible happen is a trait that resilience holds close. This student explains:

> I guess because I was very vocal and shameless, I got to stay here. I did have a semester where I could not make up the rest of my tuition and I actually went to the president and told him that I really wanted to stay and he actually gave me a grant to stay. So I guess it is what you make it.

## Conclusion

Creating a scholar begins with a parent taking the time.

Taking the time to set up a place for their child to work is important. Is it at the dinner table while you are cooking? Does your child work better on the floor with pillows? Take the time to talk with the child about school, what works and what doesn't work. Take the time to have the important conversations so the child knows their needs are important.

Creating a scholar is about the parent's intention. When the parent wants a productive, prosperous future for their child they have to show it in their actions. They can make a plan with the child to let them know that their success is the parent's success. Let the student know that you will go out of your way to attend their events. If you cannot be there in person, have someone in your place, videotape the event and share it together later.

Then finally, it does take love. Use the supportive words and gestures, refrain from physically hurtful punishments. Be creative in the corrective behavioral strategies. Parents show love differently. As long as your child can feel the love and you have put all of these other things in place, you have put yourself on the road of creating that scholar.

# Chapter 7:
# Conclusion

While the number one school factor that affects children's academic achievement is the effectiveness of the teacher, the number one out of school factor is the relationship between the parent and the child. Our research and experiences found as children move from elementary to secondary the direct teaching of skills and content by parents, decreases. This book has revealed how the parent-children relationship can positively contribute to the child's high academic achievement as long as parents continue to expect high performance, communicate goal specific academic expectations, provide emotional and financial support, meet the transportation needs of their children, and continue to advocate for an appropriate education.

We also found the parent-child relationship contributes to the ability to persist until college graduation among post-secondary students as long as the communication, support mentoring, and strategic advocacy continue. What we have attempted to do through the writing of this book is to give you practical research-based suggestions on how to raise a scholar. We began with practices for pre-school students, turned the discussion to elementary aged children, uncovered the mysteries of the adolescent student struggling to become a scholar identified the academic role of families facing parental incarceration, and concluded with the often neglected and forgotten role of parents in the academic lives of their college aged children.

In each of these chapters, you found that the message was very similar. First and foremost, the effort to raise a scholar requires your time, attention, intention, patience, persistence resilience, and love. In an often-quoted book published almost 30 years ago, Dr. Reginald M. Clark (1983) explained why poor children succeed or fail in school. He found that it did not matter how much money the household made or the education level of parents, what was most important was the value of the relationship between parents and child and the content of the conversations that occurred between them. The current research confirms this is still true today and not just for students from poor households but working- and middle-class homes as well. There are several students despite their household income or the educational level of their parents who have achieved high academic performance and are very successful and wealthy professionals. Your relationship and the content of your conversations begin with having a concrete expectation that your child will graduate from college. Once you have that expectation books like this one and people who enter your lives such as the four authors of this book, will provide you with vital information that you may not have had if you did not graduate or even attend college. You are now equipped with information. You understand the importance of communicating concrete expectations for academic excellence and the need to commit to the time and specific practices that are required to raise a scholar.

During the pre-school years, parents are the children's predominant teacher. What you choose to do with that time and what you choose to teach your child will provide either a strong or shaky foundation for your child's future school teachers to build upon. We discussed the research that uncovered a multi-million word disparity between parents who utilize a wide vocabulary and those who do not. In almost all professions, we are required to sustain our professional knowledge through continued reading and training so that we remain current in our fields. If you believe what we believe, that parenting is the most important profession that any human being can ever decide to do then it makes a great deal of sense that you continue your education, and continue reading as much as you can. The only way to ensure that your child is not on the lower side of that multi-million word gap is to constantly read, expand your vocabulary, spend quality reading and play time with your pre-schooler, and limit the amount of time you sit them in front of the TV while you complete other tasks.

As your child enters school, do not relinquish your job as teacher but begin to share it. Your job is now to encourage your child to learn. You complete this encouragement through activities such as monitoring and helping with homework. Since you know your child better than anyone else, you must reinforce the importance of high academic performance. You will model how to set priorities by instructing your child to put activities that ensure high academic achievement first, participation in extracurricular activities second, and leisure time activities last. This is accomplished through setting concrete criteria for your child to participate in performances or athletic competition and leisure time activities. You should never deny your child opportunities to work out or practice artistic and musical skills as this builds discipline and healthy habits. As one of your child's teachers, you will provide direct instruction when reviewing homework or returned examinations. When you are asked to sign an examination by your child's teacher, use this as an opportunity to review the mistakes that your child made on the test. Your responsibility as your child begins school and starts to face the obstacles that prevent him or her from high academic achievement is to maintain their self-esteem. You should be encouraging your child to achieve their personal best, by trying their hardest and learning all that they can. Finally, as a parent of an elementary school student, you must teach them to take responsibility for his or her actions despite positive or negative consequences.

The relationship that you build with your child comes from the activities and discussions that you have. These are expressions of the love that you have and communicate. There is no substitute for praises, hugs, and other affirmations of support and encouragement. As your child's first teacher, you must model positive behavior for him or her. "Do as I say not as I do" never works in the long run when raising children, and it just will not work when raising a scholar.

There are lessons that you as a parent will teach directly to your child. These lessons reflect your beliefs about hard work honesty, teamwork, risk-taking, and the value of knowledge and wisdom. Your child will encounter obstacles on the way to becoming a scholar. As a parent, it is your responsibility to ensure that these obstacles do not chip away at the self-esteem you've instilled in your child the moment they were in your arms. You must always instill a belief in your child that he or she can accomplish anything as long as he or she is willing to research and develop a concrete plan and expend the time and effort to implement this plan. Your child must always believe that despite the many obstacles that he or she will face that the ultimate outcome rests in their hands.

Children will learn to be responsible if their parents are willing to teach them. You cannot expect a responsible student who completes assignments outside of your watchful eye if you do not require your child to assume any responsibilities for their own actions and for the cleanliness of the environment in which they call home. Beginning with household chores and continuing when your child makes choices to either pursue academically rigorous coursework or artistic and athletic excellence, or even all three, the commitment level to completing the tasks necessary for high performance and positive outcomes will be demonstrated to you through the amount of time dedicated to the tasks and the amount of leisure time sacrificed.

When children are young they cannot make wise decisions for themselves so you must be steadfast and make these decisions for them. As your children mature, making the decisions for them becomes more difficult and becomes counterproductive to their growth as independent human beings. It is about the conversations you have with your children when you taught them to believe in themselves, in their abilities to achieve, and the value of dedicating one's time to the achievement of his or her goals that will prepare them to make the wise decisions.

As children mature it is important not to leave them to their own devices and continue to engage them in discussions about academics and social interactions. These conversations must be concrete by asking specific questions about courses they are taking, grades that they are achieving and projects and tests that are due. As children move from elementary to secondary school levels continue these conversations daily and weekly. These conversations need to be data-based, meaning you need to have paper that provides evidence of your child's progress and achievement.

As your child progresses to the secondary school level, he or she will be tempted to lessen their effort toward high academic achievement, especially if their chosen peers do not have the same belief about the importance of earning high grades. This cannot be tolerated. You must continue to reinforce your concrete expectations for their high academic achievement. Through this continual communication your child will understand that the grades that they receive matter and that "doing my best" but not increasing effort is unacceptable. Since secondary level education is divided into content areas such as English, mathematics, music, science, social studies, physical education, etc. you should ask for the results of examinations at least once per week. Your daily conversations with your secondary school level child should cover the learning that took place in school that day, the homework he or she has completed or needs to complete, and the progress on any projects of papers that may be due in the near future. You need to have daily conversations about the social interactions with friends and teachers. Based on these conversations, you have the responsibility to decide whether it is time to advocate for your children's best interests with middle or high school teachers and administrators or to engage in real talk about possible life-altering decisions that your child will make in the future.

While becoming increasingly difficult to supervise, you must persist in limiting the amount of time your teenage children spend alone at home, limiting the time they have for leisure activities such as television and Internet surfing, and enforcing your rules about notifying you about their whereabouts when they are away from home. Despite any resistance you must continue to have family activities together such as meals frequent conversations, and continued participation in organized youth activities. While your child may be growing bigger and taller than you, he or she still enjoys knowing that you are satisfied and pleased with their effort through praise and hugs. Even as the academic workload increases, it is important that you insist that your child complete their chores but allow them to negotiate when this completion will take place as they are juggling academic, extracurricular activity, and social schedules. This is good practice for the next step, college, and the step after that, professional life.

Children of incarcerated parents are at a disadvantage. It

is important that both the custodial and incarcerated parent work together to raise this scholar. Both sets of parents must understand that structural barriers that incarceration creates and work to ensure that there is communication between the incarcerated parent and the child. The incarcerated parent should be part of the planning and supervision as much as possible. Report cards, progress reports, and transcripts are items that the incarcerated parent should see and speak to their child about. The custodial parent should inform the child's school of the incarcerated status of the child's parent and ensure that the school communicates with this parent. Children of an incarcerated parent as well as the custodial and the imprisoned parent need to identify community organizations that will provide support socially and emotionally for the family. While the child may not see the incarcerated parent every day, it is important for that parent to be a role model of lifelong learning and continue his or her education and acquisition of knowledge during the incarceration. Even if your child is enrolled in college he or she still needs both the custodial and incarcerated parent to mentor them through the situations they encounter there. We hear many people lament on the book smarts but lack of common sense or "street smarts" their college graduates may possess. Whose fault is that if you allow incarceration to prevent you or the incarcerated parent from communicating and teaching your child these lessons?

As children move on to college these conversations become less frequent; however, they must still occur. If you pay the tuition bills, you have a right to know what you're paying for. Having your child discuss their college GPAs and their plans to improve or maintain the high average needed to meet their career goals and college graduation is your right as a parent, even if they have earned a full scholarship. Your days of supporting extracurricular activities, negotiation, and advocacy do not stop until your child has graduated with a bachelor's degree.

Your college-enrolled child still needs to know that you're going to be involved in their education. Your involvement becomes more advisory and less supervisory. You still have your expectations for high academic achievement. As a college parent you need to be available to assist your child as they encounter situations that neither of you could have expected. College will be a time where relationships are fraught with disappointment situations occur where grades will be lower than expected, and incidents with other students and college staff will be filled with misinterpretations and preconceived notions. Your child will experience newfound freedom and be tempted with alcohol drugs, and sexual situations that while present in high school will be easier to experiment in during college. The relationship and communication that you establish with your child during their pre-college years will either pay dividends or will not last the test of time. You need to keep the communication open and alive during the college years by calling, texting, and emailing frequently. It is important for your college aged child to know that he or she can count on you even if they attend school thousands of miles away. Your college-aged child must know that parents are still their strongest supporters.

Raising the scholar is hard work, but it is rewarding. As your child faces this new world where competition for employment and for customers is more fierce than ever before, it is important that your child has a plan for a prosperous future that includes high academic achievement and college completion. This book was written to give our readers concrete easy-to-follow steps to ensure high academic performance from the children. You should refer back to the practices that are listed in each chapter often.

Reading this book does not need to be the end of your journey to raise a scholar. South Shore Scholars Associates, Incorporated (SSSA) offers workshops that will allow you to share some of your best practices and listen to the best practices of other parents as they raise scholars. By visiting our website www.SSSAedconsult.com, you can become a member of our mailing list, participate in several online conversations, and be the first to be invited to upcoming presentations and workshops. At SSSA, we say, "You need a license to drive or to get married you need a certification to teach, practice law, or practice medicine; but there is no test of fitness to determine if a person is ready to have a child." We implore you to be in tip-top mental physical, social, and psychological shape as you go forth and raise your scholar.

# References

## Chapter 2

Clark, R. M. (1983). *Family life and school achievement: Why poor black children succeed or fail*. Chicago: University of Chicago Press.

Hart, B., & Risley, T. (2003). The early catastrophe: The 30 million word gap. *American Educator, 27*(1), 4–9

O'Donnell, K. (2008). *Parents' reports of the school readiness of young children from the National Household Education Surveys Program of 2007 (NCES 2008-521).*National Center for Education Statistics, Institute of Education Sciences, U.S. Department of Education. Washington D.C. Available at http://nces.ed.gov/pubs2008/2008051.pdf

Organisation for Economic Co-operation and Development. (2010). *What can parents do to help their children succeed in school? PISA in Focus 10.* Available at http://www.oecd.org/pisa/49012097.pdf

Phillips, M., Brooks-Gunn, J., Duncan, G., Klebanov, P., & Crane, J. (1998). Family background, parenting practices, and the black-white test score gap. In C. Jencks & M. Phillips (Eds.), *The black-white test score gap* (pp. 103–145). Washington, DC: Brookings Institute Press.

Pierret, C. R. (2006). *The sandwich generation: women caring for parents and children* (Monthly Labor Review). Available at U.S. Bureau of Labor Statistics website: http://www.bls.gov/opub/mlr/2006/09/art1full.pdf

## Chapter 3

Bandura, A. (1994). *Self-efficacy*. Hoboken, NJ: John Wiley & Sons, Inc.

Chavkin, N. F., & Williams, D. L. (1993). Minority parents and the elementary school: Attitudes and practices. *Families and schools in a pluralistic society, 73–83.*

Colson, M. J. (2010). *The investigation of research-based home parental involvement practices, parental style, and student achievement* (Doctoral dissertation).

EngageNY of the New York State Education Department. (2013). Available at http://www.engageny.org/sites/default/files/resource/attachments/common-core-shifts.pdf

Gardner, H. (1985). *Frames of mind: The theory of multiple intelligences.* New York: Basic Books.

Henderson, A. T., & Mapp, K. L. (2002). *A new wave of evidence: The impact of school, family and community connections on student achievement.* Austin, TX: Social/Emotional Development and Learning.

Hoover-Dempsey, K. V., & Sandler, H. M. (2005*). Final performance report for OERI Grant#R305T010673:The social context of parental involvement: A path to enhanced achievement.*Project Monitor, Institute of Education Sciences, US Department of Education

Lareau, A. (1989). *Home advantage: Social class and parental involvement in elementary education.* London: Falmer.

Muller, C., & Kerbow, D. (1993). Parent involvement in the home, school, and community. In B. Schneider & J. S. Coleman (Eds.), *Parents, and their children, and schools* (pp. 13–42). Boulder, CO: Westview.

## Chapter 4

Abboud, S. K., & Kim, J. Y. (2006). *Top of the class: How Asian parents raise high achievers—and how you can too.* New York: Berkley Books

Brown, J. C. (2010). *A case study of high-achieving Black male students and their perceptions of the causes for the Black-White test score gap in a Long Island middle school* (Doctoral dissertation).

Desimone, L. (1999). Linking parent involvement with student achievement: Do race and income matter? *Journal of Educational Research, 93*(1), 11.

Downey, D. B., Ainsworth, J. W., & Qian, Z. (2009). Rethinking
the attitude-achievement paradox among Blacks.
*Sociology of Education, 82*(1), 1–19.

EngageNY of the New York State Education Department.
(2013). Available at http://www.engageny.org/data-
driven-instruction

Friedman, T. L. (2011, November 20). How about better parents.
*The New York Times.* Available at
http://www.nytimes.com/2011/11/20/opinion/sunday/frie
dman-how-about-better-parents.html?_r=0

Glasser, W. (1965). *Reality therapy: A new approach to
psychiatry.* New York: Harper & Row.

Mandara, J., Varner, F., Greene, N., & Richman, S. (2009).
Intergenerational family predictors of the Black–White
achievement gap. *Journal of Educational Psychology,
101*(4), 867–878.

Marzano, R. J. (2000) *Transforming Classroom Grading*
Association for Supervision and Curriculum
Development...

P. McGuire. (2013, February 21). A scorecard is no way to pick
a college. [Web log post]
http://www.huffingtonpost.com/patricia-mcguire/college-
scorecard-flaws_b_2707702.html

Mickelson, R. A. (1990). The attitude-achievement paradox
among black adolescents. *Sociology of Education, 63*(1),
44–61.

National Center for Educational Statistics. (2012). *Digest of
Education Statistics: 2011.* Available at
http://nces.ed.gov/programs/digest/d11/

New York State Education Department (SED). (2012). *The New
York State Report Card 2011-12.* Available at from
https://reportcards.nysed.gov/statewide/2012statewideRC
.pdf

New York State Education Department (SED). (2009). *Guide to
grades 3-8 testing program.* Available at
http://www.emsc.nysed.gov/osa/ei/gr3-8guide10.pdf

Nurmi, J. (1991). How do adolescents see their future? A review of the development of future orientation and planning. *Developmental Review, 11*(1), 1–59.

Thomson, E., Hanson T. L., & McLanahan, S. S. (1994). Family structure and child well-being: Economic resources vs. parental behaviors. *Social Forces, 73*(1), 221–242.

## Chapter 5

Advocates for Children of New York. (2010). *Tips for working with children of incarcerated parents.* Available at http://www.advocatesforchildren.org/tracker?utm_campai gn=pdf&utm_medium=pdf&utm_source=internal&utm_ content=sites/default/files/library/tips_for_working_with _children_of_incarcerated_parents.pdf

Ardila, A., Rosselli, M., Matute, E., & Guajardo, S. (2005). The influence of the parents' educational level on the development of executive functions. *Developmental Neuropsychology, 28*(1), 539–560.

Arditti, J. A., Smock, S. A., & Parkman, T. S. (2005). It's hard to be a father: A qualitative exploration of incarcerated fatherhood. *Fathering, 3*, 267–288.

Beckert, T. E., Strom, P. S., & Strom, R. D. (2007). Adolescent perception of mothers' parenting strengths and needs: A cross-cultural approach to curriculum development for parent education. *Adolescence, 42*(167), 487–500.

Bushfield, S. (2004). Fathers in prison: Impact of parenting education. *The Journal of Correctional Education, 55*(2), 104–116.

Covington, P. (1995). *Breaking the cycle of despair: Children of incarcerated mothers.* [Brochure]. New York: Women's Prison Association & Home Inc.

Eddy J. M., & Reid J. B. (2002). The adolescent children of incarcerated parents: A developmental perspective. In J. Travis (Ed.), *Prisoners once removed* (pp. 233–252). Washington, DC: The Urban Institute Press.

Gabel, S. (1992). Children of incarcerated and criminal parents: Adjustment, behavior, and prognosis. *Bulletin of the American Academy of Psychiatry and the Law, 20*(1), 33–45.

Hoff-Ginsberg, E. (1991). Mother-child conversations in different social classes and communicative settings. *Child Development, 62,* 782–796.

Johnson, E. I. (2006). Youth with incarcerated parents: An introduction to the issues. *The Prevention Researcher, 13*(2), 3–6.

Magaletta, P. R., & Herbst, D. P. (2001). Fathering from prison: Common struggles and successful solutions. *Psychotherapy, 38*(1), 88–96.

Parke, R., & Clarke-Stewart, K., & Department of Health and Human Services. (2002, January). *From prison to home the effects of parental incarceration on young children.* Washington, DC: The Urban Institute.

Patterson, J., Mockford, C., & Stewart-Brown, S. (2005). Parents' perception of the value of the Webster-Stratton parenting programme: A qualitative study of a general practice based initiative. *Child: Care, Health & Development, 31*(1), 53–64.

Restrepo, A. (2007). *A program design: Developing the parenting skills of Hispanic incarcerated fathers.* (Unpublished doctoral dissertation). Carlos Albizu University, Miami, FL.

Seymour, C. (1998, September). Children with parents in prison: Child welfare policy, program, and practice issues. *Child Welfare, 77*(5), 469.

Smith, M. J. (2010). *Perceptions of parenting practices of incarcerated fathers who have received parent training and those who have not in a federal prison in a northeastern urban community* (Doctoral dissertation). Available at http://search.proquest.com/docview/820813131?accounti d=10549

Thombre, A., Montague, D., Maher, J., & Zohra, I. Z. (2009). If I could only say it myself: How to communicate with children of incarcerated parents. *The Journal of Correctional Education, 60*(1), 1.

Trice, A. D., & Brewster, J. (2004). The effects of maternal incarceration on adolescent children. *Journal of Police and Criminal Psychology, 19.*

Wakefield, S. (2007). *The consequences of incarceration for parents and children* (Unpublished doctoral dissertation). University of Minnesota, Minneapolis, MN.

Yearwood, E., & McClowry, S. (2008). Home is for caring, school is for learning: Qualitative data from child graduates of insights. *Journal of Child and Adolescent Psychiatric Nursing, 21*(4), 238–245.

## Chapter 6

Astin, A. W., (1984). Student involvement: A developmental theory for higher education. *Journal of College Student Development, 40*(5), 518–529.

Banning, J. H. (1978). Campus ecology: A perspective for student affairs [Monograph]. *NASPA Journal.*

Friedman, T. L., (2007). *The world is flat 3.0: A brief history of the twenty-first century.* New York: Picador.

Holmes, S. L., Land, L. D., & Hinton-Hudson, V. D. (2007). Race Still Matters: Considerations for mentoring Black women in academe. *The Negro Educational Review, 58*(1–2), 105–129.

Hurtado, S., Carter, D. F., & Spuler, A. (1996). Latino student transition to college: Assessing difficulties and factors in successful college adjustment. *Research in Higher Education, 43*(2), 163–186.

Kuh, G. D. (2001-2002). Organizational culture and student persistence: Prospects and puzzles. *College Student Retention, 3* (1), 23-29.

Miller, R. & Tatum, S. (2006). The association of family history knowledge and cultural change with persistence Among undergraduate low-income first-generation college students, *RTDE 24*(2), 41.

Swartz-Kulstad, J. L., & Martin, W. E. (2000). Culture as an essential aspect of person-environment fit. In W. E. Martin Jr. & J. L. Swartz-Kulstad (Eds.), *Person-environment psychology and mental health: Assessment and intervention* (pp. 169–195). Mahwah, NJ: Erlbaum.

Tillman, L. C. (2001). Mentoring African American faculty in predominantly White institutions. *Research in Higher Education, 42*(3), 295–325.

Tinto, V. (1993). *Leaving college: Rethinking the causes and cures of student attrition.* Chicago: University of Chicago Press

**Chapter 7**

Clark, R. M. (1983). *Family life and school achievement: Why poor black children succeed or fail.* Chicago: University of Chicago Press.